GIVE GOD A YEAR

A Yearlong Journey to Faith,
Freedom, and Fulfillment in Christ

Ben Murray

Written by Ben Murray
Copyright © 2025 Ben Murray. All rights reserved.
Published by City Hope Family, Inc.

No part of this publication may be reproduced, distributed, or transmitted in any form or by any means, including photocopying, recording, or other electronic or mechanical methods, without the prior written permission of the copyright owner, except in the case of brief quotations embodied in critical reviews and certain other noncommercial uses permitted by copyright law.

This book was written by Ben Murray and published with the support of City Hope Family, Inc., a nonprofit organization. The funding and resources for this work were generously provided by City Hope Family, Inc., as part of its mission to inspire and equip individuals to grow in their faith and personal development.

All Scripture quotations, unless otherwise indicated, are taken from the Holy Bible, New International Version® (NIV®) Copyright ©1973, 1978, 1984, 2011 by Biblica, Inc.® Used by permission. All rights reserved worldwide.

Additional Scripture quotations are used by permission as follows:

New Living Translation (NLT), ©1996, 2004, 2015 by Tyndale House Foundation.

New American Standard Bible® (NASB), ©1960, 1971, 1977, 1995, 2020 by The Lockman Foundation.

THE MESSAGE (MSG), ©1993–2002 by Eugene H. Peterson, NavPress.

The Living Bible (TLB), ©1971 by Tyndale House Foundation.

Hardback ISBN: 979-8-218-66805-1
Paperback ISBN: 979-8-218-60958-0
LCCN: 2025903822

In collaboration with
WestSky Publishing
www.westsky.studio/publishing

To my family—Annaliese, my constant encourager, and our four incredible boys, Garrett, Gavin, Gideon, and Gibson. You are my greatest joy and my legacy. My prayer is that you always chase after God with everything in you.

To the people of City Hope Church—you inspire me daily with your faith, generosity, and passion for Jesus. It is an honor to walk this journey with you.

And to every reader—this book is an invitation. An invitation to trust God, to surrender fully, and to step into a life you never imagined possible. My prayer is that as you give God a year, He will give you more than you ever dreamed in return.

TABLE OF CONTENTS

Foreword 1
Introduction 5
Chapter 1 | Jesus Is Lord 7
Chapter 2 | The Power (and Positivity) of Repentance 15
Chapter 3 | Your New Family 23
Chapter 4 | Why Church? 31
Chapter 5 | First Things First 41
Chapter 6 | The Heart Test 51
Chapter 7 | Relationship not Works 57
Chapter 8 | God Time 63
Chapter 9 | What is the Bible About? 71
Chapter 10 | A Firm Foundation 79
Chapter 11 | Who is the Holy Spirit? 87
Chapter 12 | An Empowered Life 95
Chapter 13 | Making Prayer Personal 103
Chapter 14 | Finding Freedom 113
Chapter 15 | Your Identity, Your Giftings, and Your Purpose . . 119
Chapter 16 | 3 Keys for Healthy Relationships 127
Chapter 17 | Get in a Small Group 137
Chapter 18 | How to Love 143
Chapter 19 | The Dream Team 151
Chapter 20 | Choose Joy 159
Your Next Step 167

FOREWORD

You won't know what God has to offer until you go all in.

I've been reminded of this truth again and again throughout my life. And my firm belief in it is not based on my experience—it's based on the promise in God's Word: "You will seek me and find me when you seek me with all your heart" (Jeremiah 29:13, NIV). The more I've surrendered all areas of my life to God, the more I've been surprised to see Him working in ways beyond my wildest dreams.

I believe in this promise so much that I frequently share it when I preach and teach. Initially in a sermon at the beginning of the year, I remember asking, "What would you have to lose if you gave God a year? What would happen if you went all in and faithfully followed Him in every area of your life?" I challenged people to become as active in church as possible, attending every weekly service, participating regularly in a small group, reading their Bible daily, making prayer part of everything they did, serving others the way Jesus served everyone He encountered during His time on earth. I said, "If your life hasn't changed dramatically at the end of that year, then I'll change churches with you!"

This offer might sound like a joke, but I meant it. Because the promise in Jeremiah makes it clear. If you don't give your all, it won't work and you won't find God. A trickle of faith won't work—you must open the floodgates. A sideline spectator kind of faith doesn't work either—you have to get in the game and run the play. If you want to know God, you can't be incremental or halfway. He wants your whole heart and promises you will find Him when you hold nothing back and give Him 100%.

I often share this challenge with other pastors attending our GROW conferences—the annual events we host to connect, encourage, and help leaders and their churches reach their full potential. Which is where my friend Ben Murray heard me say it. He loved the simplicity and directness of the invitation to "give God a year and watch what He'll do." So Ben began challenging everyone at his church to do the same and was amazed at what happened.

People took to heart the challenge to give God a year and couldn't believe the results. Just as people often come up to me and describe what happened during their year, Ben began hearing similar testimonies. People would share about how God worked in their lives from the inside out. They described drawing closer to God like never before, of marriages miraculously healed, families reunited, addictions defeated, and discovering their divine purpose. They connected more deeply in their relationships and experienced new levels of peace and joy in their daily lives.

It's not easy but it is simple. Throughout the pages of the Bible, God reveals how we can be who He created us to be, how we can know the life of abundance His Son came to bring—if we're willing to obey His Word and follow the example Jesus set for us. While there is no magic formula or failproof system, there are spiritual practices and personal adjustments we can make that are guaranteed to change us.

After witnessing such incredible outcomes when people were willing to give God a year, Ben was inspired to write this book. I loved the idea of extending the life-changing impact of this challenge and encouraged him to go for it. Throughout the following pages, you will find a cumulative and collective resource that's sure to strengthen your faith and enrich your life. Drawing on the timeless truth of Scripture, the perfect example of Jesus, and insightful illustrations from his own life, Ben shares how anyone and everyone can experience dramatic growth in just one year.

Few books excite me like *Give God a Year*. And I'm humbled and delighted that my tendency to repeat what I know to be true ignited the same kindred passion in my friend, Ben. If you feel stuck in place or just want to continue the momentum toward maturity in your faith, this book will become one you will read and return to again and again.

My prayer is that you would experience the same joy, peace, and sense of purpose that God wants you to have.

But you must be willing to go all in. If you will surrender your life and commit to loving and following God for an entire year, then you will not be where you were when you started. You will not be *who* you were when you started.

Do you want to become more of who God made you to be?

Do you wish you could experience a deeper, more intimate relationship with the Lord?

Do you need to break free of old habits and lingering wounds from the past?

Do you long to know unshakable peace and abiding joy day-in and day-out?

Then your next step is clear.

Give God a year!

—Chris Hodges
Founding Pastor, Church of the Highlands
Author of *Out of the Cave* and *Pray First*

INTRODUCTION

Congratulations! I'm so thrilled this book has found its way into your hands. No matter where you are in your journey with God, He has more for you. Life with Him isn't about arriving at a final destination, it's about the ongoing adventure of walking with Him daily. Along the way, there's always room for growth, opportunities to learn, and ways to become more like Jesus.

I'd be honored to be a friend and guide on this journey.

Now, imagine this with me: we're sitting together over a cup of coffee, having a heartfelt conversation about what's next in your spiritual walk. You've made the decision to follow Christ—whether that was yesterday or years ago—and now you're ready to go deeper. There's a spark of excitement, mixed with a bit of nervousness, as you consider the possibilities.

We talk about your hopes, your dreams, and your desire to experience more of God. You tell me about the questions stirring in your heart: Where do I start? What steps do I take? How do I live for Him every day?

And as we finish our conversation, I offer you this simple answer: Give God a year.

This book is my way of showing you what that looks like—step by step. Together, we'll explore practical, life-giving ways to deepen your relationship with God, align your life with His purpose, and grow in faith. My hope is that by the end of this year, you'll look back and see undeniable evidence of God's work in your life.

I won't promise that everything will be perfect. Life has its challenges, and following Jesus doesn't make those disappear. But I can promise this: as you lean into this process, stay faithful, available, and teachable; you will be transformed. A year from now, you'll see a version of yourself that's more alive, more joyful, and more connected to the heart of God than ever before.

So, let's dive in. It's time to give God a year and see what He will do in and through your life.

CHAPTER 1

JESUS IS LORD

"Isn't Dad the first person you want to meet when you get to heaven?"

I was twelve when I asked my mom that question. I was seven when my dad passed away.

Alone. Grieving. Widowed. My mom wasn't given a choice when she became a single parent.

It was heartbreaking and confusing; you can fill in the blank with any negative emotion. We were there. And I remember living there for years. Yet through it all, three words marked my childhood and were the hallmark of my mom's journey.

Jesus is Lord.

I would see those three words scribbled on notes everywhere. In the bathroom. On the fridge. In my mom's notebook. On the coffee table. In the car.

Jesus is Lord.

My mom was a single parent for five years until she remarried. And I remember one day in particular that will be etched in my memory forever.

I was twelve years old and struggling. I missed my dad. That's when I asked her, "Don't you miss him? Isn't Dad the first person you want to meet when you get to heaven?" Her answer shocked me.

"No."

"What? Why? Who else could it be?"

Her answer hurt my feelings. Didn't she love him? Why doesn't she miss him like I do?

Mom led me through the sliding glass door to our patio. She sat me down, looked me directly in the eye, and shared that when she was younger she had two abortions.

"Those are the first people I want to see when I get to heaven."

I'll never forget that conversation. My mom had a past I didn't know about. Jesus wasn't always her Lord, but when she married my dad, they got radically saved. Their lives—and life together—transformed.

When she would write on all those pieces of paper, "Jesus is Lord," it wasn't a trivial or legalistic phrase. Those words were real to her. They were alive. They were a testament to what Jesus had done and continued to do in and through her life.

Jesus became her Lord. Jesus is mine.

Is He yours?

Giving God a year of your life begins with making him the Lord of your life.

Before we take another step on this journey, it's critical you make this decision for yourself. Romans 3:23 (Holy Bible, New International Version) says, "for all have sinned and fall short of the glory of God ..."

John 3:16 reads, "For God so loved the world that he gave his one and only Son, that whoever believes in him shall not perish but have eternal life."

Romans 10:9 tells us, "If you declare with your mouth, 'Jesus is Lord,' and believe in your heart that God raised him from the dead, you will be saved."

So often, we focus on Jesus as our Savior, and He is! When He died on the cross and rose again, He bore our sin and shame, paying the debt we never could so we can be reunited with God and receive the gift of eternal life. But it's also important to realize we're not only meant to invite Jesus to be our Savior. We're also to declare with our mouths, "Jesus is Lord."

Now, perhaps you're wondering, What does that mean? I thought "Lord" was only used in England in the 1800s! In the original Greek language that the New Testament is written in, "Lord" means "Master."[1] It's someone who has absolute ownership rights over a given person.

In other words, and in the context of this book, it's surrendering control to God. It's going all in.

Giving God a year of your life is saying to Jesus, "I not only believe You're my Savior and rose from the dead. I'm giving You control of my life. All that I am is Yours, forever!"

That may sound dramatic. And to be honest, it is. But I promise you, it's the best decision you will ever make.

Jesus is good. Jesus is loving. Jesus is gracious. Jesus doesn't wield His authority like a taskmaster. He watches over you as a shepherd, leading you to rest, empowering you with strength, and providing for you every step of the way.

Psalm 23 is a beautiful passage of scripture. Even if you didn't grow up attending church, you may have heard it referenced by a friend or someone in a movie. Right now, I want to encourage you to read it in light of making Jesus your Lord.

Read it to discover His heart towards you. Read it as you receive His unconditional love for you. Let it permeate every part of who you are.

> [1]The Lord is my shepherd; I have all that I need. [2]He lets me rest in green meadows; he leads me beside peaceful streams. [3]He renews my strength. He guides me along right paths, bringing honor to his name. [4]Even when I walk through the darkest valley, I will not be afraid, for you are close beside me.

---

1   G2962 - kyrios - Strong's Greek Lexicon (kjv)." Blue Letter Bible. Web. <https://www.blueletterbible.org/lexicon/g2962/kjv/tr/0-1/>. Accessed 6 Dec, 2024.

Your rod and your staff protect and comfort me. ⁵You prepare a feast for me in the presence of my enemies. You honor me by anointing my head with oil. My cup overflows with blessings. ⁶Surely your goodness and unfailing love will pursue me all the days of my life, and I will live in the house of the Lord forever. (Holy Bible, New Living Translation)

There's a story in scripture about Peter, one of Jesus' disciples. It was the day of Pentecost. Many of Jesus' followers who had seen Him die and then witnessed His resurrection gathered in an "upper room" to receive the gift Jesus promised before He ascended—the Holy Spirit (Acts 2:1).

(Note: I'll share more about the Holy Spirit in a later chapter. Trust me, you don't want to miss it. This Christian life isn't possible without Him!)

The Holy Spirit comes upon these followers of Jesus, and it causes such a ruckus that people outside the building thought they were drunk! So, Peter responds. He preaches a short message to the few thousand gathered outside and ends it with these words:

> '³⁶Therefore let all Israel be assured of this: God has made this Jesus, whom you crucified, both Lord and Messiah.' ³⁷When the people heard this, they were cut to the heart and said to Peter and the other apostles, 'Brothers, what shall we do?' ³⁸Peter replied, 'Repent and be baptized, every one of you, in the name of Jesus Christ for the forgiveness of your sins. And you will receive the gift of the Holy Spirit. ³⁹The promise is for you and your children and for all who are far off—for all whom the Lord our God will call.' ⁴⁰With many other words he warned them; and he pleaded with them, 'Save yourselves from this corrupt generation.' ⁴¹Those who accepted his message were baptized, and about three thousand were added to their number that day. (Acts 2:36–41)

I love that story. It's such a great example of what it means to make Jesus your Lord and what happens as a result.

JESUS IS LORD

There will be many more times I refer to Peter throughout this book but make no mistake, Peter would not have been capable of speaking those words in and of himself.

This was a man who put his foot in his mouth a lot. He cut a Roman soldier's ear off because he was overly zealous to protect Jesus. Then, hours later, he denied Jesus three times, right after Jesus prophesied that would happen and Peter promised it wouldn't!

That Peter surrendered control. And what God did through him continues to impact the world today. But none of that would have been possible had Peter not made Jesus his Savior and Lord.

Now, I must confess that while I'm sharing with you the importance of recognizing the Lordship of Jesus, I realize it's something easier said than done. Human nature doesn't like to be told what to do. We want to be in the driver's seat. We want to do things our way.

But, I wonder, how has that worked out for you? Are you at peace? Fulfilled? Do you know your purpose? I don't ask these questions to condemn you. I ask these questions because they're ones I've asked myself when I've lost sight of Jesus as my Lord.

If you're reading this book, I have a hunch you're ready to stop holding so tightly to your way and start letting Jesus have His way in and through you.

It's amazing to note that for Peter and all those first-century believers referred to in the book of Acts, declaring Jesus as Lord had the potential of being a death sentence. The same word used for "Lord" was the same used for "Caeser Hail Caeser," the Roman Emperor.[2]

When someone said, "Caeser Hail Caeser," they declared he had supreme authority. But when someone said, "Jesus is Lord," they stated that He was above Caesar. At that time in history, that was a big deal!

---

2   Little, Jeff. The Way to Win. Blount Collective, 2021. Pg. 82.

"Jesus is Lord" was a life-threatening phrase. Thankfully, for those of us here in America, stating such words carries no threat of persecution and punishment. However, it can mean the difference between life and death. It can mean the difference between a life of shame and regret or redemption and restoration.

It did for my mom.

As a child, I never would have thought she had skeletons in her closet. I never imagined she would have anything in her past that could have the potential to carry such condemnation.

If not for Jesus. By making Him her Lord, not only did she find purpose for the future, but she also experienced forgiveness for her past.

I want that for you—today and for the rest of your life. I want you to experience the transformation and enduring hope that comes from surrendering completely to the Lordship of Jesus Christ.

I want you to commit to giving Him the final say in your life. Even when it doesn't make sense. Even when you don't understand it. Even when you can't comprehend it.

Trust His Word, His will, and His way. You won't be perfect. You're going to make mistakes, and that's okay. Nevertheless, draw a line in the sand today that you're going to give this one-year challenge a try.

Give God a year of your life. Decide to follow Jesus no matter the cost or inconvenience. Make this your prayer as it is mine:

> "I'm ready to give my life to Jesus. Forgive me of all my sins. Make me new. From this day forward, I choose to follow you. I want to fall in love with you. I commit myself to living for you, serving you, and loving you with all my heart. Amen!"

Remember, making Jesus your Lord means you won't keep living the way you have been. A change is happening. A process of transformation is beginning. It's the first step on our journey together, and it inevitably leads to the next step. Something that involves the most positive word in the Bible, though admittedly, you may disagree with me at first!

GO ALL IN

- When you've heard someone say "Jesus is Lord" in the past, what have you thought?
- How has your perspective of those words changed after reading this chapter?
- What is one aspect of Jesus' nature that encourages you after reading Psalm 23?
- Is there a hurt from your past that makes it hard to trust others? Remember Psalm 23. That's your Savior and your Lord. He won't fail you. He won't forsake you. He will always love you and care for you!

CHAPTER 2

THE POWER (AND POSITIVITY) OF REPENTANCE

I just wanted a burrito. You wouldn't expect that to stir up trouble on a quiet city street, but I quickly learned that's not the case—especially when you're driving the wrong way!

My wife, children, and I had recently moved back to Wichita Falls, TX, to plant a new, life-giving church called City Hope. I was no stranger to this city. It's where my wife and I met and married.

One morning, not long after we moved, I woke up craving a burrito from The Burrito Shop. The only problem was that I forgot the road to get there was one-way.

I'm driving and all these people are waving at me. *Good to see you too!* I think. They keep waving. I wave back. Their kindness touches me until I realize why they're waving.

I drove the wrong way for half a mile!

Thankfully, I didn't run into another car and I didn't get a ticket. Here's my point: I thought life was good until I realized I was going the wrong way. I needed to do a U-turn. I needed to change direction.

I needed to repent.

More on that word in a moment, but let me be clear: when you receive Jesus as your Lord and Savior, your eternal destiny instantly changes. That's salvation. But your life's circumstances and situations remain. Temptations and difficulties still happen.

There's a responsibility to face the life you've been living and the sinful capacities you've formed. Yes, you're going to heaven, but you still might have some battles on this earth. That's where repentance comes in and the process of sanctification, which is a word to describe the transformation God brings about in your life. Think of it this way ...

Salvation is the decision.

Sanctification is the process.

Repentance keeps you moving forward.

When Jesus spoke of repentance, scripture recorded it as the Greek word metanoia meaning "a change of mind" (Matt. 9:13).[3]

Repentance isn't bad. Repentance isn't dirty. Repentance doesn't involve you beating yourself up nor is it an attempt to prove how sorry you are. It isn't even a promise to God that you'll never do anything wrong again.

Repentance is a change of mind. In my opinion, it's the most positive word in the Bible because it's the act of realizing you've been heading in the wrong direction and need to turn back to God.

The question you might be asking at this point, however, is: how? If salvation is a one-time decision and sanctification is a process that involves repentance, what does that practically look like?

A humorous yet effective example would be that it looks like a man driving to get a burrito when suddenly he realizes he's driving the wrong way and changes his direction!

Jesus said, "What good will it be for someone to gain the whole world, yet forfeit their soul? Or what can anyone give in exchange for their soul?" (Matt. 16:26).

---

[3] G3341 - metanoia - Strong's Greek Lexicon (kjv)." Blue Letter Bible. Web. <https://www.blueletterbible.org/lexicon/g3341/kjv/tr/0-1/>. Accessed 5 Dec, 2024.

THE POWER (AND POSITIVITY) OF REPENTANCE

The Apostle Paul, someone who persecuted Christians until he had his own U-turn experience said, "I preached that they should repent and turn to God and demonstrate their repentance by their deeds" (Acts 26:20).

Unrepentance is a lifetime of pain. Being repentant is a moment of pain. It can hurt to realize you've been wrong and hurt even more if what you've done has negatively affected others. It's what many refer to as Godly sorrow. But it doesn't bring condemnation.

"Therefore, there is now no condemnation for those who are in Christ Jesus" (Rom. 8:1).

That's you! Godly sorrow is simply a solemn realization that change needs to happen.

We're human and imperfect. Sanctification doesn't happen in an instant. It's part of overcoming. It's part of transforming. It's part of becoming who God created you to be so you can do what He's calling you to do.

Sanctification, at its simplest definition, means to let God work some bad things out of you and some good stuff into you.

Following Jesus doesn't mean a life without mistakes, but it can mean a life without regrets.

There was a man in the Bible named David who excelled at repentance—mostly because he messed up a lot! He was the King of Israel, somebody God referred to as a man after His own heart (1 Sam. 13:14). Yet he also had a high capacity for sin.

Exhibit A: He had an affair with one of his closest friend's wives. Then, she got pregnant. Then, he had that friend killed. Then, because of David's actions, the son dies. Talk about a mess! But David repents. And we find his repentant response to God in Psalm 51 …

For the director of music. A psalm of David. When the prophet Nathan came to him after David had committed adultery with Bathsheba. ¹Have mercy on me, O God, according to your unfailing love; according to your great compassion blot out my transgressions. ²Wash away all my iniquity and cleanse me from my sin. ³For I know my transgressions, and my sin is always before me. ⁴Against you, you only, have I sinned and done what is evil in your sight; so you are right in your verdict and justified when you judge. ⁵Surely I was sinful at birth, sinful from the time my mother conceived me. ⁶Yet you desired faithfulness even in the womb; you taught me wisdom in that secret place. ⁷Cleanse me with hyssop, and I will be clean; wash me, and I will be whiter than snow. ⁸Let me hear joy and gladness; let the bones you have crushed rejoice. ⁹Hide your face from my sins and blot out all my iniquity. ¹⁰Create in me a pure heart, O God, and renew a steadfast spirit within me. ¹¹Do not cast me from your presence or take your Holy Spirit from me. ¹²Restore to me the joy of your salvation and grant me a willing spirit, to sustain me. ¹³Then I will teach transgressors your ways, so that sinners will turn back to you. ¹⁴Deliver me from the guilt of bloodshed, O God, you who are God my Savior, and my tongue will sing of your righteousness. ¹⁵Open my lips, Lord, and my mouth will declare your praise. ¹⁶You do not delight in sacrifice, or I would bring it; you do not take pleasure in burnt offerings. ¹⁷My sacrifice, O God, is a broken spirit; a broken and contrite heart you, God, will not despise. ¹⁸May it please you to prosper Zion, to build up the walls of Jerusalem. ¹⁹Then you will delight in the sacrifices of the righteous, in burnt offerings offered whole; then bulls will be offered on your altar. (Psa. 51:1–19)

Psalm 139 is another beautiful Psalm that David wrote. While it isn't a psalm of repentance, it provides us with a powerful pattern to pray. He says, "**Search me**, God, and **know my heart; test me** and know my anxious thoughts. See if there is any offensive way in me, and **lead me** in the way everlasting" (Psa. 139:23–24, emphasis added).

Here's the pattern:

THE POWER (AND POSITIVITY) OF REPENTANCE

- Search me—We will always be as sick as our secrets. So, ask God to search you: Is there anything in my life that isn't like You?
- Know Me—God knows you better than you know yourself. Allow Him to reveal the true motives of your heart. Ask God to know everything about you: Is there anything I'm hiding?
- Test Me—As God reveals anything hidden within you, He's going to allow you to experience situations that test you. Ask God: Is there anything You want to do in and through me?
- Show Me—If we let Him, God will show us the areas of our lives that need to change. He will send the Holy Spirit to convict us of sin and righteousness.
- Lead Me—God's leadership is perfect. Proverbs 3:5-6 says He will make our paths straight if we trust Him. So, ask God to lead you and be quick to follow Him.

To give God a year of your life means following that pattern. It means to go all in.

As we've already discovered, the goal isn't perfection. But I can promise you, as you continue taking each step on this journey, you won't recognize yourself. Your life will be different. Your life will be better, regardless of the circumstances around you because you'll know and grasp the love, grace, and power of the One who is within you!

Now, before we move on from this chapter, I want to touch on another powerful act that follows salvation and exemplifies repentance: water baptism.

Repentance is part of the transformation Jesus brings within us. Water baptism is its outward representation. It isn't a ritual, ceremony, or celebration of doing the right thing. It's a public, outward expression of inward change.

When the Bible was written, and even to this day, Jewish synagogues have a mikvah—a small pool of water. A mikvah has seven steps leading down into a baptism pool, and it serves as a purification ritual for anyone considered "unclean."

I mention that because the practice of water baptism isn't something the modern-day Christian Church came up with. It's something the Israelites did. And it's something John the Baptist was doing in Jesus' day.

In Matthew 3 we find him baptizing people in the Jordan River. "I baptize you with water for repentance. But after me comes one who is more powerful than I, whose sandals I am not worthy to carry. He will baptize you with the Holy Spirit and fire" (Matt. 3:11).

Later, we find the story of when Jesus came to John to be baptized: "John tried to deter him, saying, 'I need to be baptized by you, and do you come to me?' Jesus replied, 'Let it be so now; it is proper for us to do this to fulfill all righteousness.'" Then John consented (Matt. 3:14–15).

Why did Jesus need to be water baptized? He didn't have sin in his life. He didn't need to repent of anything. He was water baptized as an example for us and to identify with us.

I also want to pause for a moment and highlight what happened after Jesus was baptized.

As soon as Jesus was baptized, He went up out of the water. At that moment heaven was opened, and he saw the Spirit of God descending like a dove and alighting on him. And a voice from heaven said, "This is my Son, whom I love; with him I am well pleased" (Matt. 3:16–17).

Until that point in His life, there were no recorded miracles of Jesus. The Bible simply says that as a child He grew in wisdom and stature and in favor with God and men (Luke 2:52). That's it.

Jesus hadn't turned water into wine, healed anybody, gone on the forty-day fast, or sacrificed Himself on a cross. Yet, before Jesus did anything noteworthy, God declared for the world to hear, "This is my Son. With Him, I am well pleased".

Do you need to hear that today? Maybe you don't feel close to God. Perhaps you've made Him Lord of your life recently, but you've been caving into your old ways. Or you've been a follower of Christ for years and trying to live a life that pleases Him, but you're filled with doubt and shame for all the times you've messed up.

Friend, God isn't pleased with you because of your actions. Of course, He loves it when you follow His Word and ways. But He loves you for YOU and is pleased with you because of who and Whose you are!

God is intimately aware of how you've been made, what you've done, and what you will do. Still, He loves you. He's proud of you for accepting Jesus as your Lord and Savior and choosing to repent of the way you've been living. I believe He's excited that you're reading this book!

We say it this way at City Hope Church, "God loves you just as you are, but doesn't want you to stay as you are."

Paul writes something significant in Romans 6:1–4: "¹What shall we say, then? Shall we go on sinning so that grace may increase? ²By no means! We are those who have died to sin; how can we live in it any longer? ³Or don't you know that all of us who were baptized into Christ Jesus were baptized into his death? ⁴We were therefore buried with him through baptism into death in order that, just as Christ was raised from the dead through the glory of the Father, we too may live a new life."

An old song refers to water baptism as a water grave. Just as Christ was raised from the dead by God, we're raised to new life in Christ when we come out of that water. The struggle, however, is that the day-to-day can still be a challenge.

We face temptations and trials. The old sinful nature rears its ugly head. Paul writes in the next chapter, "For what I want to do I do not do, but what I hate I do" (Rom. 7:15).

Remember, we're human. Mistakes are a part of life. Sanctification is a process. But because Jesus is your Lord, He calls the shots now. If you take a wrong step, repent. Change direction. Let God's kindness lovingly bring you back to what's right and the good things He has for you (Rom. 2:4).

When I was driving to get that burrito, I didn't realize I was driving the wrong way until I arrived at my destination, the burrito shop. I would have repented and changed course sooner if I had realized. But here's the reality: life doesn't always have that clear of a destination.

Every day, keep giving God permission to transform you into who He made you to be. As you repent, God will change the way you think. As He changes how you think, He'll change how you act. And as He changes how you act, you'll know God's will for you is good, pleasing, and perfect.

We don't always know where we'll end up in life. We don't always know what's right and wrong. We can, however, receive direction for the next step. We never have to go on this journey alone. And that's what we'll discover more about in the next chapter.

GO ALL IN

- How have you experienced repentance in your life?
- Is God calling for you to make a U-turn even now in a specific area or situation?
- Have you been water baptized? If so, what was your experience like? If not, do you feel like God is calling you to this next step?

CHAPTER 3

YOUR NEW FAMILY

Imagine yourself in the heart of the African savanna.

Amidst the landscape, you see a lion crouching. Its eyes are locked on its target—a gazelle that strayed too far from its family and herd. Among the hundreds, this one is vulnerable because it's alone.

The tension mounts. The lion closes in. Finally, it bursts into action, its intention propelling it forward with lethal precision. The chase is swift, a blur of motion and instinct.

The lone gazelle never stood a chance.

Now, if you're wondering why I started this chapter like a scene from a National Geographic documentary, here's why: "Your enemy the devil prowls around like a roaring lion looking for someone to devour. Resist him, standing firm in the faith, because you know that the family of believers throughout the world is undergoing the same kind of sufferings" (1 Pet. 5:8–9).

Our enemy is the devil. He's a defeated foe Jesus conquered on the cross. But he's still out for blood on the earth. He's seeking to steal, kill, and destroy (John 10:10). Not exactly a declaration for world peace, right? And if you live an isolated life–devoid of family or community–you're setting yourself up to be attacked.

I lived in Alabama for a time with my family and I'll never forget seeing a billboard on I-65, a beautiful stretch of road between Montgomery and Birmingham.

Beside a pristine lake and a lovely property, a sign displayed these (admittedly) head-turning words ...

Go to church or the devil will get you.

There are a lot of well-meaning Christians who might say or share things like that, which can come across as judgmental and rude. So, I want to be clear: I don't want to condemn any person or claim that they're headed for disaster if they're not part of a church. However, I do want to point out that while the enemy is defeated, he's still prowling.

For that reason, I want to share with you the value, priority, and power of embracing the spiritual family you're now a part of as a believer in Christ. And that's the church!

I'll cover the action of attending church in the next chapter. Right now, I want to touch on what your church family is biblically.

Let's look at its first mention in scripture. Studying the Bible this way is called the "Law of First Mention."

In Matthew 16:18 Jesus says, "I will build my church, and the gates of Hades will not overcome it." Clearly, Jesus started the church. It's a spiritual family. It was His idea and He takes it personally.

But the church isn't an organization. Jesus isn't talking about a beautiful cathedral where people come to hear a teacher every Sunday. To understand what Jesus is saying, we must uncover the original intent of the word "church."

The Greek word for church is *ekklēsia*, which means, "a calling out."[4] In other words, we have been called out of one thing and into another for a greater purpose in the Kingdom of God.

What have we been called into exactly? Our good friend, Peter, makes it clear. We've been called "out of darkness into his wonderful light" (1 Pet. 2:9).

---

4   G1577 - ekklēsia - Strong's Greek Lexicon (kjv)." Blue Letter Bible. Web. <https://www.blueletterbible.org/lexicon/g1577/kjv/tr/0-1/>. Accessed 5 Dec, 2024.

We'll discuss how God has called you specifically later in this book when we talk about spiritual gifts. Right now, I want you to grasp that your church family is defined by the people rather than the place.

We need each other. And we're better together. Here are just a few benefits of this spiritual family:

- We strengthen each other.

"Therefore encourage one another and build each other up, just as in fact you are doing" (1 Thess. 5:11).

- We encourage each other.

"…not giving up meeting together, as some are in the habit of doing, but encouraging one another…" (Heb. 10:25).

- We protect each other.

"Though one may be overpowered, two can defend themselves" (Eccl. 4:12).

- We help each other.

"Two are better than one, because they have a good return for their labor: If either of them falls down, one can help the other up" (Eccl. 4:9–10).

- We grow with each other.

"And let us consider how we may spur one another on toward love and good deeds…" (Heb. 10:24).

- We can correct each other.

"Let the message of Christ dwell among you richly as you teach and admonish one another with all wisdom through psalms, hymns, and songs from the Spirit, singing to God with gratitude in your hearts" (Col. 3:16).

Each of those things is a positive attribute of embracing your new family, the church. However, our personal experiences of family can also affect our perspective, beliefs, and ability to connect with others.

Family can have a lot of connotations and meanings. Not every family gets along. Not every family thrives. A lot of families fight. Some don't fight fair. No family is perfect. But a good, healthy family isn't devoid of struggle or disagreements. It's one that's committed to loving, serving, giving, and growing no matter what.

I believe the church I pastor—City Hope—is perfect for imperfect people. It's full of people, myself included, who don't have it all together but are committed to growing closer to the Lord.

We're all in. We've repented and are moving in the direction God is leading us.

That's what church—your new family—is. And whether we like it or not, it's something Jesus Himself instituted. The lack of a perfect church isn't an excuse to not be part of one.

I am the church. YOU are the church. Yes, Sundays are a day of worship when Christians attend church. But ultimately, we are the church!

Here's how I often remind my congregation at City Hope of this truth: The church is not FOR us. We ARE the church and we are here for those who aren't here yet.

So, how do I get closer to my church family?

The most important key is showing up. It's going to church any time the doors are open. Again, I'll speak more to this in the next chapter but here, I want to touch on your personal experience of family growing up. Because one inevitably affects the other.

Here are some reasons you might be skeptical of your spiritual family—

Perhaps you've been hurt

Past experiences of pain within a family or church setting can create deep wounds, making it difficult to trust again. You might hesitate to engage fully with a new family for fear of further pain. Healing begins with acknowledging this pain and seeking God's help. Psalm 147:3 assures us, "He heals the brokenhearted and binds up their wounds."

Perhaps you hold back

Fear of rejection or judgment can cause many to withhold themselves from fully engaging with others. This hesitation often stems from past experiences where openness led to criticism or indifference. If you've experienced this, I'm so sorry you've suffered that pain. Still, I believe God has so much more He wants to do in and through you as you connect with your new family!

Perhaps you self-protect

Self-protection can hinder genuine connections and growth with others. While constructing emotional barriers may have kept you from getting hurt in the past and provided a sense of safety, they also prevent the richness of shared experience. They can isolate you from the community meant to support and uplift you.

One time I was speaking to a woman who was going through a difficult season. Her husband passed away unexpectedly; then she found herself having to care for her ninety-four-year-old father alone.

As you can imagine, this woman was in a season she never expected, with unforeseen struggles and an uncertain future. But here's what she told me, "I'm so thankful for my church family. I don't know how someone could go through this without one."

She said this because her "new family members" brought her meals for two weeks. She said this because people kept showing up, asking if there was anything they could do to help. She said this because she didn't have to go through that season alone. She had a family to support and encourage her!

Being part of your new church family doesn't mean it will be perfect. Rather, being part of this family means we're doing life together.

Some people might say, "I can be the church at home." After all, since the COVID-19 pandemic of 2020, you can watch nearly any preacher or teacher you want online.

For many, live streaming a church service is their preferred "church attendance." They watch from the comfort of their place (whether in their home, office, car, etc.) and never enter the doors of a church building.

The problem with this approach is that Jesus started the church. The church and Jesus are inseparable. And while the church is defined by the people, the church is also the place we gather. If we avoid the place altogether, we're avoiding the people—the family—we're called to be in relationship with!

It would be like someone saying, "Ben, we want to invite you to our house for dinner, but we don't want your family to come. We can't stand your kids and wife. We only want to have you over."

I can't speak for Jesus, but I'm not going to any event where my family isn't welcome. If someone doesn't love my family, then how can they love me?

The best way to love someone is by loving the people they love.

Jesus loves the church. He sacrificed Himself for the church. Needless to say, it's a safe bet that loving Jesus means loving His family–His church!

Are you ready to embrace your new family? Are you committed to going to church? We're about to fully dive into what that means because when it comes to your relationship with God, going all in requires nothing less.

When it comes to giving Him a year of your life, church is an essential part of it. But I encourage you not to attend church out of an obligatory spirit. Go to church because you love God. Go because you want to grow in your relationship with Him.

There may be some days you're tired and want to stay home. There may be moments when connection is complex. Nevertheless, be committed to not isolating yourself.

Don't put yourself in a position to be attacked. Set yourself up for success and relationship with God and others. It's the next step on your journey!

GO ALL IN

- Do you find yourself feeling spiritually isolated, like a lone gazelle? What steps can you take to connect more deeply with your new family?
- Have you experienced hurt within your family or church that makes it difficult to trust and connect with others? How can you seek healing from God to overcome this pain?
- What steps can you take to invest relationally with your new church family? Are there specific individuals you can reach out to for support, friendship, or mentorship?

CHAPTER 4

WHY CHURCH?

Several years ago, I joined a mission team heading to a remote village in Mexico called Huancito. Our job was simple: Build a small side room for a local church, which included an exterior wall and foundation.

I had no idea what I was in for.

On the first day, we dug a trench two feet wide and three-and-a-half feet deep—by hand. The next day, supply trucks arrived, but they couldn't get closer than fifty yards from the church. We had to carry all the sixty-pound bags of concrete and sand to the site—by hand.

There was also a massive pile of small boulders that were just as heavy, and we had to move those too. You guessed it–by hand!

I asked Martin, our host from the church, "What are these rocks for?" He replied, "These are for the foundation." As someone lacking construction experience, I didn't fully understand, but I followed his lead.

We first placed the big rocks in the trench, then filled the gaps with smaller rocks. When we needed even smaller rocks, we used a sledgehammer to break bigger ones down.

Once the rocks were in place, we mixed and poured the concrete to cement them together. After the foundation was set, we started laying bricks for the exterior wall.

Now, we're spoiled in America. We have machines that can dig foundations in minutes and transport materials easily. But not in Huancito. Or so I thought!

Later, I asked Martin, "Do you guys have access to concrete mixers?"

"Oh yes, we do."

I was puzzled.

"We could have rented that equipment to speed things up." Martin chuckled. "We wanted you to work like we work!"

What does this have to do with the church? Well, when I think of that experience, it reminds me of a conversation Jesus had with Peter.

> ¹³When Jesus came to the region of Caesarea Philippi, he asked his disciples, 'Who do people say the Son of Man is?' ¹⁴They replied, 'Some say John the Baptist; others say Elijah; and still others, Jeremiah or one of the prophets.' ¹⁵'But what about you?' he asked. 'Who do you say I am?' ¹⁶Simon Peter answered, 'You are the Messiah, the Son of the living God.' ¹⁷Jesus replied, 'Blessed are you, Simon son of Jonah, for this was not revealed to you by flesh and blood, but by my Father in heaven. ¹⁸And I tell you that you are **Peter**, and on this **rock** I will build my church, and the gates of Hades will not overcome it (Matt. 16:13–18, emphasis added).'

Notice the two words I bolded in the passage: Peter and rock. To understand the depth of what Jesus is saying, we need to do some—excuse my dad joke–digging.

Remember, the New Testament was written in Greek. So, let's do a word study to see if we can better grasp this scripture.

The Greek word for Peter is *petros*. It means "a rock or stone."[5]

The Greek word for rock in this passage is *petra*. It's similar, but again, different. *Petra* refers to a rock, ledge, or cliff.[6] The inferred

---

5   G4074 - petros - Strong's Greek Lexicon (kjv)." Blue Letter Bible. Web. <https://www.blueletterbible.org/lexicon/g4074/kjv/tr/0-1/>. Accessed 5 Dec, 2024.

6   G4073 - petra - Strong's Greek Lexicon (kjv)." Blue Letter Bible. Web. <https://www.blueletterbible.org/lexicon/g4073/kjv/tr/0-1/>. Accessed 5 Dec, 2024.

meaning is a foundation slab. It's the kind of rock you can build something on. It's what the team and I used to make the foundation in Huancito.

I like to think that Jesus was saying, "Peter, you are an important part of what I'm doing, but you can't do it all. This whole thing can't be built on you. You're a rock among many rocks. I'm calling you to be a part of the foundation I can build on. And the enemy won't overcome it!"

I believe Jesus' words to Peter are His invitation to you. Whether Jesus and His church are new to you or familiar, He's inviting you to enjoy the blessing and community of your new family and be a rock He can build on.

Jesus is inviting you to be someone He can work through to do extraordinary things for His Kingdom. But it happens in and through His church! That's why church is such a big deal and should matter to anyone who has made Jesus their Lord.

Perhaps unsurprisingly, "Why should I go to church?", is one of the most often asked questions posed to me over my years in ministry. My answer usually consists of the following words: We are the small rocks and boulders mentioned by Jesus in Matthew 16:13–18. By ourselves, we can't do much. But together we can become a strong foundation the gates of hell can't defeat.

Now, the Bible notably describes the church as the body of Christ (1 Cor. 12:27). Let's look at what the Apostle Paul writes concerning this—

> [12]Just as a body, though one, has many parts, but all its many parts form one body, so it is with Christ. [13]For we were all baptized by one Spirit so as to form one body—whether Jews or Gentiles, slave or free—and we were all given the one Spirit to drink. [14]Even so the body is not made up of one part but of many. [15]Now if the foot should say, 'Because I am not a hand, I do not belong to the body,' it would not for that reason stop being part of the body. [16]And if the ear should

say, 'Because I am not an eye, I do not belong to the body,' it would not for that reason stop being part of the body. [17]If the whole body were an eye, where would the sense of hearing be? If the whole body were an ear, where would the sense of smell be? [18]But in fact God has placed the parts in the body, every one of them, just as he wanted them to be. [19]If they were all one part, where would the body be? [20]As it is, there are many parts, but one body. [21]The eye cannot say to the hand, 'I don't need you!' And the head cannot say to the feet, 'I don't need you!' [22]On the contrary, those parts of the body that seem to be weaker are indispensable, [23]and the parts that we think are less honorable we treat with special honor. And the parts that are unpresentable are treated with special modesty, [24]while our presentable parts need no special treatment. But God has put the body together, giving greater honor to the parts that lacked it, [25]so that there should be no division in the body, but that its parts should have equal concern for each other. [26]If one part suffers, every part suffers with it; if one part is honored, every part rejoices with it. Now you are the body of Christ, and each one of you is a part of it (1 Cor. 12:12–26).

Here are three takeaways from that passage—

Every part of the body is needed

When City Hope first started meeting as a church, we held services at a local middle school. Every week, we had to set up and take down all of our equipment, which was stored in a fifty-three-foot semi-trailer. It wasn't easy. There was a lot to keep track of, a lot to organize, and a lot to put in place. But our team had a phrase that carried us through, and it's one you may have heard before—many hands make light work. We need to be part of a team. And in that team–or body–YOU are needed. You have a unique purpose and crucial role to play in the body of Christ!

Every part of the body is necessary

The body of Christ can't accomplish as much without your participation. Don't believe me? "If one part suffers, every part suffers with it; if one part is honored, every part rejoices with it. Now you are the body of Christ, and each one of you is a part of it (1 Cor. 12:27)." Your involvement in church is necessary for the body to work as God designed it to.

Every part of the body must be developed

In the same way a newborn baby develops abilities to thrive independently as it grows, we must develop the gifts and talents God has given us. And do you know where that happens? In church with our church family!

Proverbs 27:17 says, "As iron sharpens iron, so one person sharpens another." In other words, we're better together! The very nature of the word church is plural.

Years ago, I came across a church sign that said,

Ch_ _ch

What's missing?

u r

I don't know if anyone has ever decided to go to church because they saw a sign like that. But as silly as it sounds, it's true. Here are a few next steps for gathering together:

1. Actively attend and participate in your local church.

Do you think your life would be better if you attended church faithfully fifty-two times a year for the rest of your life?

Notably, a research organization called the Blue Zone Project did a study on people who have lived more than a hundred years.[7]

They discovered that all but five of the two-hundred-and sixty-three centenarians interviewed belonged to some faith-based community. Denomination didn't seem to matter. Additionally, they found that attending faith-based services four times a month would add four to fourteen years of life expectancy.

Now, I'm not trying to convince you to attend church just by reason of living longer. It's simply worth noting that being in a community makes a difference.

Ask yourself: If I went to church, would I be closer to God?

Like anything in life, we prioritize what's important. Being part of a church can change your life if you go all in, so be committed to attending weekly, not once a month or only on holidays.

Be there every time the doors are open. Sometimes, you might miss it due to sickness, vacations, or other personal reasons. But those moments should be the exception, not the rule.

If you want to slim down in weight or bulk up your muscles, it won't happen by going to the gym or eating a healthy meal once a month. It's going to happen when you prioritize its importance in your life daily and weekly.

So, get serious about church. Make it a priority to attend, but don't stop there. At some point, you'll also need to move from being a spectator to a participator, which means …

2. Become a member of your local church.

City Hope Church offers a three-week introductory class called Growth Track. It's the pathway to getting involved.

---

[7] Felicis, Johnaé De. "The Halo Effect of Sacred Spaces." https://www.bluezones.com/2022/07/the-halo-effect-of-sacred-spaces/ . Accessed 5 Dec, 2024.

In step one, we talk about vision, values, church governance, finances, and church membership. It's a great way for people to discover who we are and if we're the right church for them.

While many other churches no longer do church membership, I still believe in it. Church membership isn't a matter of salvation and it doesn't get you any kudos with God. But it is a statement of commitment to the body of believers in your community.

Every church and their membership process is different. But for us at City Hope, church membership is saying—

I will protect the unity of my church by:

- Acting in love toward other members.
- Refusing to gossip.
- Following the leaders.

I will share the responsibility of my church by:

- Praying for its growth and health.
- Inviting the unchurched to attend.
- Warmly welcoming those who visit.

I will serve the ministry of my church by:

- Discovering my gifts and talents.
- Using my God-given gifts to make a difference in the lives of others.
- Developing a servant's heart.

I will support the testimony of my church by:

- Attending church and small groups faithfully.
- Living a Godly life.
- Giving regularly.

Becoming a member of your church helps you move from spectator to participator. Then, you can be a contributor. You can use the spiritual gifts and abilities that are needed within your local church. This leads us to the third thing …

3. Life change happens through small groups.

I can't speak to other churches but if you came to City Hope long enough, you'd hear statements like—

- Life change happens in the context of community.
- Life change happens in circles, not rows.
- Don't do life alone.
- God never promised we wouldn't suffer, He just promised we wouldn't have to suffer alone.
- We're better together.
- You'll always be as sick as your secrets.

The important thing to note about all those statements is that most happen in the context of small groups.

A small group isn't just a friend group. It's an integral part of your spiritual journey because it's a place for you to be known and loved personally by others. And it's hard for a person to be known if people aren't given the chance to know them.

Sunday service is an awesome place to gather with other believers, worship God, serve others, and listen to teachings about God's Word. But when you're confronted by daily life Monday through Saturday, it's vital to be part of a small group and intentionally invest in relationships with others.

Experiencing a life-giving community will ultimately help you settle the past and find hope for your future!

We'll dive deeper into the topic of small groups in a later chapter but for now, if you want more information about joining a small group, talk to the leaders in your church family.

Remember, the church is more than a place. Yes, it's a building where people like you and me gather, but it doesn't matter whether the building is an abandoned gas station, warehouse, storefront, school, or cathedral with a steeple.

What the building looks like has nothing to do with "the church."

An early church martyr named Stephen said, "The Most High does not live in houses made by human hands" (Acts 7:48). 1 Corinthians 3:16 further tells us, "Don't you realize that all of you together are the temple of God and that the Spirit of God lives in you?"

Friend, you are the place God wants to live in.

You are the person God wants to restore, redeem, and bless others through. Embracing your new family and going to church are essential to experiencing that reality.

But as I already mentioned when speaking about the importance of small groups, daily life doesn't start and end with Sunday service. It's on Monday, Tuesday, Wednesday, Thursday, Friday, and Saturday when you face life's challenges, setbacks, and opportunities.

If you're wondering how to step into each of those days with a deeper faith and a more grounded perspective, I have something special to share with you in the next chapter.

GO ALL IN

- Do you ever hold back from engaging with your church community due to fear of rejection or judgment? How can you lean on God's acceptance to build trust and openness?
- How consistent are you in attending church? What steps can you take to prioritize church attendance in your life?
- Are you attending church services as a spectator, or are you actively participating and contributing to the life of your church? How can you continue to engage with your church community and be part of the foundation God can build on?

CHAPTER 5

FIRST THINGS FIRST

Growing up in the small town of Sweetwater in East Tennessee was an adventure wrapped in contradictions. While sprawling shopping malls and sun-kissed beaches required a long-distance drive or flight, we were blessed with a majestic sight of our own—the Appalachian Mountains. Also affectionately called the "Smokies."

If you're from the area, I'm sure you know what I'm referring to. If you're not, picture this: whether at sunrise or sunset, you see what looks like a mist or haze in the distance. It mingles with the peaks. It dances among the trees. It nestles along the ridgeline against the backdrop of a dazzling sun.

The mountains look "smoky" which is how they get their nickname, and the beauty is captivating.

Interestingly, the Bible has a compelling story about a man with a smoky mountain experience. Only his encounter with God far surpassed the majesty of the Appalachians.

This person's name was Moses. God worked through him to lead the Israelites out of slavery in Egypt. And on a mountain called Sinai, amidst smoke, thunder, and lightning, God wrote the Ten Commandments on two stone tablets.

If you grew up in church or recited them at school, you're probably familiar with them. In this chapter, I want to focus on the first two. Here's how God describes them in Exodus 20:2–3,

"[2]I am the Lord your God, who brought you out of Egypt, out of the land of slavery. [3]You shall have no other gods before me. ⁴You shall not make for yourself an image in the form of anything in heaven above or on the earth beneath or in the waters below. ⁵You shall not bow down to them or worship them; for I, the Lord your God, am a jealous God …" (Exo. 20:2–5).

Clearly, God isn't satisfied with second. He wants to be first. He deserves to be first. He needs to be first. Because when He's first, everything else in life comes into order.

In Matthew 6:33 Jesus says, "But seek first his kingdom and his righteousness, and all these things will be given to you as well."

Now, I'm not implying that everything will be perfect when you put God first. Jesus famously said, "In this world you will have trouble"(Jn. 16:33).

Challenges will come. Setbacks will arise. But how would you prefer to go through trouble—with everything in order or out of order in your life?

Right after Jesus assured us of trouble, He encouraged us to take heart. He declared, "I have overcome the world" (Jn. 16:33). The key to seeing the reality of that promise played out is putting Him first in every area of your life—

- First in your time.
- First in your treasure.
- First in your talents.

I'll speak more to those three categories in a moment, but Jesus' words in Matthew 6:33 and John 16:33 aren't only promises for your future. They're a statement about your reality today.

Putting God first isn't a religious ritual. It's a life-giving, life-altering decision. And we don't only find this principle in Matthew, John, or on a smoky mountain in the book of Exodus. We see it at the very beginning of creation in Genesis.

"¹Adam made love to his wife Eve, and she became pregnant and gave birth to Cain. She said, 'With the help of the Lord I have brought forth a man.' ²Later she gave birth to his brother Abel. Now Abel kept flocks, and Cain worked the soil. ³**In the course of time** Cain brought some of the fruits of the soil as an offering to the Lord. ⁴And Abel also brought an offering—fat portions from some of **the firstborn of his flock**. The Lord looked with favor on Abel and his offering, ⁵but on Cain and his offering he did not look with favor" (Gen. 4:1–5, emphasis added).

Abel was a rancher and Cain was a farmer. At that time, their economic system revolved around what they did. Their income was what they grew.

Their offerings to God reflected that, and there are four lessons we can learn from their story.

#1. The first is a sacrifice

Putting something or someone first inherently costs something because other things must make space for it.

In the story, Abel's offering was a sacrifice. It cost him something—fat portions from some of the firstborn in his flock (Gen. 4:4). But Cain's was different.

We're not given specifics on what he gave but scripture is clear God wasn't satisfied with it. It wasn't a sacrifice. Cain simply gave in the course of time (Gen. 4:3).

Thankfully, the Bible provides a more thorough explanation in Jude. "Woe to them! They have taken the way of Cain; they have rushed for profit into Balaam's error; they have been destroyed in Korah's rebellion" (Jd. 1:11).

Notice how Jude likened Cain to two men–Balam and Korah. They were both well-known for their rebellious and greedy actions.

Similarly, Cain wanted more (greed) and to do things his way (rebellion). However, I don't believe his greed or rebellion was overt or boisterous. If anything, it may have been all too similar to you and me.

Perhaps he thought, "Man, I've been working hard. God, You're not the one who's doing all this work. I'll give something to You, but I also have a right to enjoy what I've got." I think we can all relate to having thoughts like that. But Cain didn't just think that. He acted on it.

Instead of bringing God a selfless offering, he brought something selfish.

Here's the second lesson from this story, which concerns Abel's offering specifically—

#2. The first takes faith

When you don't know what will happen the rest of the year, it takes faith to sacrifice the firstborn of your flock. After all, for a rancher, that's their livelihood. It's everything. Maybe Abel was even thinking, "Am I going to have enough for the rest of the year? God, this hurts."

Those are feelings we can relate to as well.

When you can't see if the car will break down, if the washer will stop working, or if that business opportunity will fall through, yet you put God first anyway. You give something to Him, whether it's financial or otherwise.

You see, this principle of putting God first is a principle of trust. Remember those three categories I shared earlier? Here's what they look like practically—

- **Your time.** This can be waking up and giving God the first few minutes of your day by praying, worshipping, and reading His Word. Even when you've got a project pressing on your mind. Even when the house is a mess. Even when you're tired and don't feel like it. (Speaking from experience here!)

- **Your treasure.** This could be the tithe, a type of giving we find throughout scripture where God asks us to give Him the first ten percent of our income. I want to emphasize though that God doesn't need our money. He's doing fine, trust me! The point isn't the amount or the percentage. The point is the principle. The point is putting Him first, before paying bills or anything else.
- **Your talents.** Whether you're gifted in business, music, or sports, you can submit your dreams and goals to God and ask Him what He wants you to do with them.

It's what Abel did.

"[1]Now faith is confidence in what we hope for and assurance about what we do not see. [2]This is what the ancients were commended for. [3]By faith we understand that the universe was formed at God's command, so that what is seen was not made out of what was visible. [4]By faith Abel brought God a better offering than Cain did. By faith he was commended as righteous, when God spoke well of his offerings. And by faith Abel still speaks, even though he is dead" (Heb. 11:1–4).

Abel didn't just give anything to God. He sacrificed. He put Him first. And God commended him for it; "And by faith Abel still speaks, even though he is dead."

When you put God first in every area of your life, you will experience financial, emotional, and physical blessings. You will also leave a legacy for generations to come!

This leads us to the third lesson to learn—

#3. The first honors God

Proverbs 3:9–10 says, "Honor the Lord with your wealth, with the firstfruits of all your crops; then your barns will be filled to overflowing, and your vats will brim over with new wine."

What would honoring God with the firstfruits of your income look like for you? I want to be clear: this isn't a principle based on opinion. This is grounded in God's Word. Plus, there's a promise!

The first isn't meant to be discarded or used without a thought. The first is fit for a king. Abel recognized this and so can we. Now, let's go back to Genesis and look at what else happened after they gave God their offerings.

> "⁴The Lord looked with favor on Abel and his offering, ⁵but on Cain and his offering he did not look with favor. So Cain was very angry, and his face was downcast. ⁶Then the Lord said to Cain, 'Why are you angry? Why is your face downcast? ⁷If you do what is right, will you not be accepted? But if you do not do what is right, sin is crouching at your door; it desires to have you, but you must rule over it'" (Gen. 4:4–7).

If you believe God is quick to anger and lacking in grace, you might read those words and think God is giving Cain a hard time.

If you had a parent who punished you before they heard you, God might seem the same way. But God isn't quick to anger; He's slow to it (Psa. 86:15). He chooses mercy over judgment (Jam. 2:13). We love Him because He first loved us (1 Jn. 4:19).

In that passage, we can mistakenly see God talking down to Cain when He's trying to help him.

Let me paraphrase what He said: "Cain, why are you angry? Why are you upset about this? Why are you sad and depressed? It's going to be okay. If you do what's right, I will accept your offering. But I need to warn you. If you keep putting Me second and won't let Me be the Lord of your life, sin is crouching at your door. And it wants to have you. It wants to manipulate you. It wants to own you. This is why you must rule over it."

Do you see God's kindness in those words? Remember, His kindness (not judgment or punishment) leads us to repentance (Rom. 2:4). This brings us to the fourth lesson to learn—

#4. Putting God first is the right thing to do

Abel chose the right thing. Cain chose the wrong thing. Abel chose God's way. Cain chose his way. And while God gave Cain the opportunity to choose rightly next time—which He always does—Cain didn't get better. He got bitter.

When we get bitter at God, we get bitter at others. They get blessed and we can't stand it. They experience good things and we hate them because of it.

Tragically, we see this progression in Cain's story: "Now Cain said to his brother Abel, 'Let's go out to the field. While they were in the field, Cain attacked his brother Abel and killed him (Gen. 4:8)."

The story of Cain and Abel is a profound example of what can happen when you choose or refuse to put God first in your life.

Remember, the blessing God releases when you put Him first isn't merely a promise. It's reality. And I could share with you story after story from my life and in the lives of people I know who've experienced this firsthand. Here's one of them in their own words …

My husband John and I visited Wichita Falls (WF) for the first time in August, 2022. We had some friends in the area, found a house, and the adventure began. The process of giving God a year started without me knowing it. That is how our Jesus works! On the way home [one day], we saw City Hope. I saw many people, flags waving, and a man putting his little one in the car. I said to John we needed to try this church. On our first visit, I had tears in my eyes as the music began. On my prayer card, I asked that I would find connections with wonderful women. Well, Jesus answered that prayer and then some. I attended 21 Days of Prayer. After week two, I met some wonderful friends. One day, I had a lunch date and a nail appointment date on the same day! I was invited to dinner with a small group of ladies. More connection! In October, John had a mild stroke. All the folks I met were ready and waiting to help in any way. I was super excited to get into a small group. I am also part of the prayer, greeter, and worship teams. At the Freedom Conference, I asked for healing from celiac disease. It took some time for me to believe in healing, but by February, I was done dealing with celiac and accepted that I was healed. It has been a good year. My heart has been open, and Jesus has filled it with more than I could have imagined!

Isn't that testimony amazing? Are you ready to put God first? In the context of our church community at City Hope, this is what putting God first looks like …

- **We give God the first of our day.** This can include reading the Bible, worship, and prayer.
- **We give God the first of our month.**
  - » We tithe. We set aside the first ten percent of our increase and entrust it to God, His Kingdom, and the church. Again though, the tithe isn't about the percentage. It's the principle. It's honoring God first with our first!
  - » First Wednesday. We dedicate the first Wednesday evening of every month to a time of community, worship, and teaching from God's Word.
  - » First Saturday. We put God first by putting others first. On the first weekend of each month, we set aside the first Saturday to serve our community in any way we can.
- **We give God the first of our year.**
  - » Every January, my church family and I go on a twenty-one-day prayer and fasting journey. Together, we commit to putting God first and believing Him to move in and through us in awesome ways.

Putting God first is about so much more than money. Ultimately, He wants your heart because it's from your heart that every area of your life overflows.

The question is, does He have it? Even if it meant giving Him the one thing—or person—that meant the most to you?

I ask because God requested this of Abraham in the Bible. The story is shocking. The action God asks of him seems cruel. But in the end, something beautiful, powerful, and promising happens that means everything for you and me.

GO ALL IN

- Think about how you currently prioritize God in your daily life. What practical steps can you take to ensure God is first in your time, treasure, and talents? How might this shift in focus bring more order and peace to your life?
- Reflect on the role of faith in putting God first. How can you cultivate greater trust in God when making decisions, especially when the future is uncertain? What might be holding you back from fully trusting Him with everything you have?
- How does the story of Cain and Abel resonate with you? Are there areas of bitterness or resentment affecting your relationship with God or others?

CHAPTER 6

THE HEART TEST

There are some wild stories in the Bible.

- A man gets swallowed up by a whale and lives to tell the tale (Jon. 1:17).
- There's a donkey that talks (Num. 22:8).
- A meal is served to a Prophet by ravens (1 Kings 17:2–6).
- An apostle is bitten by a poisonous snake and does not suffer one side effect (Acts 28:3–6)!

Needless to say, following God can mean a life full of unexpected moments, unforeseen challenges, and miraculous breakthroughs.

That's why I'm so grateful this book is in your hands.

I'm excited you've taken on this challenge to give God a year of your life. There's no telling all the wonderful things God has in store for you! However, there are some key steps on this journey and another story in the Bible reveals the next one before us.

In the previous chapter, we talked about the principle of the first, which matters in every area of life—your time, talent, and treasure. It's trusting God with it all. But doing so is ultimately an issue of the heart; that's where trust starts.

I don't think anything can test a heart more than sacrificing your only child.

Now, please stay with me because if you're not familiar with this story, you might be tempted to freak out. As I just mentioned, the Bible has some WILD stories, and this is undoubtedly one of them.

"Some time later God tested Abraham. He said to him, 'Abraham!' 'Here I am,' he replied. Then God said, 'Take your son, your only son, whom you love—Isaac—and go to the region of Moriah. Sacrifice him there as a burnt offering on a mountain I will show you'" (Gen. 22:1–2).

God knew what He was doing.

First of all, He would never have anyone kill or sacrifice a child in His name. That's not what He does, and it isn't who He is. But in the time and culture in which the book of Genesis took place, child sacrifice was a heartbreakingly normal practice.

Not everyone worshipped or followed the one true God. People would build idols. They'd make up gods. And they'd institute disgusting, heart-wrenching, murderous practices as part of their distorted religions.

Abraham was aware of this. Abraham had seen this. And I wonder if a part of him wondered if this God, who promised to make his descendants numerous and blessed, was different (Gen. 12:1–3).

So, God tested his heart. Not merely to reveal who Abraham was at his core but to reveal who God Himself was, is, and always will be.

Here's the rest of the story …

> ³Early the next morning Abraham got up and loaded his donkey. He took with him two of his servants and his son Isaac. When he had cut enough wood for the burnt offering, he set out for the place God had told him about. ⁴On the third day Abraham looked up and saw the place in the distance. ⁵He said to his servants, 'Stay here with the donkey while I and the boy go over there. We will worship and then we will come back to you.'
>
> ⁶Abraham took the wood for the burnt offering and placed it on his son Isaac, and he himself carried the fire and the knife. As the two of them went on together, ⁷Isaac spoke up and said to his father Abraham, 'Father?' 'Yes, my son?'

Abraham replied. 'The fire and wood are here,' Isaac said, 'but where is the lamb for the burnt offering?'

⁸Abraham answered, 'God himself will provide the lamb for the burnt offering, my son.' And the two of them went on together. ⁹When they reached the place God had told him about, Abraham built an altar there and arranged the wood on it. He bound his son Isaac and laid him on the altar, on top of the wood.

¹⁰Then he reached out his hand and took the knife to slay his son. ¹¹But the angel of the Lord called out to him from heaven, 'Abraham! Abraham!' 'Here I am,' he replied. ¹²'Do not lay a hand on the boy,' he said. 'Do not do anything to him. Now I know that you fear God, because you have not withheld from me your son, your only son.'

¹³Abraham looked up and there in a thicket he saw a ram caught by its horns. He went over and took the ram and sacrificed it as a burnt offering instead of his son. ¹⁴So Abraham called that place The Lord Will Provide. And to this day it is said, 'On the mountain of the Lord it will be provided.'

¹⁵The angel of the Lord called to Abraham from heaven a second time ¹⁶and said, 'I swear by myself, declares the Lord, that because you have done this and have not withheld your son, your only son, ¹⁷I will surely bless you and make your descendants as numerous as the stars in the sky and as the sand on the seashore.

Your descendants will take possession of the cities of their enemies, ¹⁸and through your offspring all nations on earth will be blessed, because you have obeyed me.' (Gen. 22:1–18)

Isaac was Abraham's first and only son.

Isaac was already a miracle because Abraham's wife Sarah was past child-bearing age when she had him. To Abraham, he was an answer to prayer—the fulfillment of God's promise. And yet, God was asking him to sacrifice him.

Talk about a test! But for you and me on this side of the cross, we can learn that God will never ask you to do something He's not already done. Why? Because the first redeems the rest.

Look at Exodus 13 with me. This is after Abraham and Isaac. This is after God gave Moses the Ten Commandments. Exodus 13:1–2 says, "The Lord said to Moses, 'Consecrate to me every firstborn male. The first offspring of every womb among the Israelites belongs to me, whether human or animal.'"

Later, we read, "...you are to give over to the Lord the first offspring of every womb. All the firstborn males of your livestock belong to the Lord. Redeem with a lamb every firstborn donkey, but if you do not redeem it, break its neck. Redeem every firstborn among your sons (Ex. 13:12–13)."

God gets the first. The Israelites keep the rest. And it's all blessed because of it. Why? Because it goes back to the heart.

- Cain didn't give the first, and it revealed his heart. There was greed, rebellion, and a lack of faith and trust in God.
- Abel gave the first. God could see Abel's heart was in the right place. So, He accepted his offering and blessed it.
- Abraham was willing to put God first in an incredible act of trust and God provided for him.
- God gave His first–Jesus–and now, you and I are redeemed because of it!

Exodus 13 describes how there were clean animals (e.g. lambs), and unclean animals (e.g. donkeys).

In essence, every year, the Israelites had to sacrifice a spotless (or perfect) lamb to cleanse the people of their sins. This was an "atoning" sacrifice. But then there were unclean animals.

Whenever an unclean animal was born, such as a donkey, if a person wanted to keep it, they had to sacrifice a clean lamb in its place—otherwise, bye-bye, donkey.

To live, it had to be redeemed.

Here's why I share all that with you: We are the unclean. Jesus is the clean!

The only reason we can be here is because the perfect, sinless, spotless lamb of God slain before the foundations of the world was sacrificed in our place.

Let me put it this way: Jesus is God's tithe! Jesus is God's first and best. Because of God's great love for you and me, He sacrificed His firstborn, even while we were still willing to act like Cain. Even though we were hesitant to give Him our whole heart.

Why? So we might be saved, redeemed, and restored to Him. That's good news! And many scriptures testify to this. Here are a couple of examples—

> "But Christ has indeed been raised from the dead, the firstfruits of those who have fallen asleep. For since death came through a man, the resurrection of the dead comes also through a man" (1 Cor. 15:20–21).

> "The Son is the image of the invisible God, the firstborn over all creation" (Col. 1:15).

Remember, God wouldn't ask something of you before doing it Himself. We love because He first loved us. We give because He first gave.

Knowing this, I encourage you to trust Him. Give Him your heart and don't hold anything back. He won't abandon you. He won't fail you. He won't forsake you. Put Him first, give Him a year of your life, and be amazed at all He will do in and through you!

I want to pose a question to you now, as we take the next step on our journey together. And before you turn the page, I encourage you to consider your answer.

Perhaps you already know what the answer is, biblically. Regardless, the answer is absolutely critical to know, believe, and live out.

What does God want from you?

GO ALL IN

- Think about the story of Abraham and Isaac. Are there areas in your life where God might be testing your faith in Him? How can you demonstrate a deeper trust in God's provision, even when the outcome is uncertain or challenging?
- Consider what you are willing to sacrifice for God. Is there something in your life you're holding onto tightly, perhaps fearing what might happen if you let it go? How can you practice offering your "first" to God, whether it's time, talent, or treasure, and trust Him to bless the rest?
- How do your actions and priorities reveal the condition of your heart? Are there any changes you need to make to ensure your heart is aligned with God's and that He is truly first in your life?

CHAPTER 7

RELATIONSHIP NOT WORKS

Okay, here's the question: What does God want from you?

There's your time, talent, and treasure as we learned about in the chapter covering the principle of first. God wants those things, right?

There's your obedience—your ongoing commitment to follow God and do everything He says.

There's your future—your hopes and dreams.

There's your money, work, mind, and of course, your heart.

There are a lot of possible answers. Ultimately, however, there's one answer we need to recognize and understand. It will make every part of giving God a year so much better. And we find it in Luke 10, in a story about two sisters, Mary and Martha.

Jesus was visiting their home. It was unexpected and a huge event for a small village outside of Jerusalem. People were coming from all over to hear Him teach. And they didn't even have social media to get the word out!

Martha, the older sister, busied herself with preparations. She worked tirelessly. Her mind raced with making food for the guests, keeping the place clean, and ensuring everyone's needs were met.

A few steps away, her sister Mary sat at the feet of Jesus. If she had given any thought to preparations, she dismissed them. Her heart and spirit were captivated by Jesus' words.

Martha was getting overwhelmed. She wanted her sister's help, and understandably so. Finally, her frustration grew until she could bear it no longer.

"Lord, don't you care that my sister left me to do the work alone? Tell her to help me!" (Lk. 10:40)

Jesus' response is stunning. He doesn't respond to Martha's plea with rebuke. He speaks with compassion.

"'Martha, Martha,' the Lord answered, (repeating someone's name in scripture was a sign of deep care and empathy) 'you are worried and upset about many things, but few things are needed—or indeed only one. Mary has chosen what is better, and it will not be taken away from her'" (Lk. 10:41–42).

Here's the lesson: The value of being in Jesus' presence far outweighs the busyness of life. Even busyness that's rooted in serving Him.

What Jesus wants from you isn't what you can do for Him. He wants *you*!

No doubt we can easily find ourselves like Martha, caught up in the demands of life—oftentimes good and necessary things.

Still, if we're not careful, they're things that can pull us away from living in God's presence and experiencing an intimate and fulfilling relationship with Him.

No doubt there's a lot that goes into following Jesus. After all, we're only in chapter seven of twenty in this book!

But this story sets a vital precedent we must recognize before focusing on other things we might want to or need to do.

God desires relationship with you before anything you can do for Him. And up until we decide to receive Jesus as our Savior and make Him our Lord, we are practicing a way of life that isn't what God designed us for.

Perhaps you practiced earning the approval of others.

Maybe you practiced some habits–drinking, smoking, pornography, overeating–that helped you cope with pain.

Maybe you practiced doing life on your own, refusing to accept help from anyone.

Giving God a year of your life means letting go of your old way of life and its practices.

The Apostle Paul writes in this context, "Finally, brothers and sisters, whatever is true, whatever is noble, whatever is right, whatever is pure, whatever is lovely, whatever is admirable—if anything is excellent or praiseworthy—think about such things. Whatever you have learned or received or heard from me, or seen in me—**put it into practice**. And the God of peace will be with you" (Phil. 4:8–9, emphasis added).

Paul understood this principle of practice. Before he was saved, he persecuted Christians. Talk about a lifestyle change!

But notice what Paul, even as he busied himself with everything God was calling him to do, remained focused on:

> "I press on to take hold of that for which Christ Jesus took hold of me. Brothers and sisters, I do not consider myself yet to have taken hold of it. But one thing I do: Forgetting what is behind and straining toward what is ahead, I press on toward the goal to win the prize for which God has called me heavenward in Christ Jesus" (Phil. 3:12–14).

What's the prize? Life with Jesus. Nothing more. Nothing less.

Please hear my heart: I don't want you to see this book as a list of rules, religion, and duties with a bunch of boxes to check.

We call what Jesus did on the cross a finished work because that's precisely what it is, finished! The blood of Jesus saves you through your faith in Him.

The key to practicing this new way of life isn't only about what we do—though, again, our actions are important. This Christian life is ultimately about relationship, not works.

It's about loving God and being loved by Him because your behavior will naturally align with what your heart treasures most.

(Remember, just like the principle of the first!)

The phrase "fall in love" is often tossed around in today's culture. Personally, I'm not a big fan of it because it sounds accidental.

In reality, love is a choice. It requires intentionality. It's the fertile framework for any healthy relationship. And here's a benefit: When we're in love with God, we won't feel like we *have* to do what He says. We *get* to do it.

If you give God a year from the starting point of only doing the right things, it will inevitably get old and exhausting. But when you receive God's love and love Him, everything changes for the better.

You understand how He sacrificed His one and only Son to save you. And you love Him.

You recognize all the ways He's protected and provided for you throughout your life when you didn't realize it. And you love Him.

You recall the dreams, purpose, and promises He's placed in your heart. And you love Him.

Then, you follow Him. You want to obey Him. You want to do what He says because you know He has your best at heart.

1 John 5:3 tells us, "In fact, this is love for God: to keep his commands. And his commands are not burdensome …"

In the next chapter, we're going to get practical about one specific quality every good relationship has. But before we get there, I want to share with you the moment loving God became real for me.

I was sixteen when I bought my first Bible. I still have it and cherish it because of how God has spoken to me through it. But when

I started reading, when I began prioritizing my relationship with God and giving Him my life, I came upon Psalm 63.

"You, God, are my God, earnestly I seek you; I thirst for you, my whole being longs for you, in a dry and parched land where there is no water (Psa. 63:1)."

That was the cry of my heart as a sixteen-year-old.

As I shared with you earlier in this book, I had witnessed firsthand what God did in my mom's life, how He had redeemed and restored her as she made Jesus her Lord and Savior.

I'm grateful for her example. It ministered to me. And as I read more of the Bible, He became my first love (Rev. 2:4).

While I've gone through seasons when I've lost sight of Him, when my relationship with Him became routine, I'm grateful that I've returned. I've repented. I've gone back to the principle of practice, remembering God wants me more than anything I can do for Him.

Will you receive that truth today? Will you remember to focus on relationship, not works?

Let me encourage you to serve God out of delight, not duty. If you enjoy it, you won't have to endure it, and that's a powerful thing!

We're about to dive into some practical parts of being a Christian, of giving God a year of your life and some keys to doing that on a daily basis. Each of these keys is beneficial. Each of them will help you live a more hopeful, encouraged, and empowered life.

But as you read about them and start applying them, don't forget to let them be an overflow of relationship. It's about getting to do these things, not out of obligation, but love.

We've covered a lot of ground in these first seven chapters. We've made Jesus Lord, repented, embraced our church family, and got our priorities straight. We're putting first things first—God!

But it's time to talk about what comes next. It's time to form some habits to make this whole "Give God A Year" thing even better.

GO ALL IN

- What do you believe God wants most from you at this stage in your life? How does it align with the story of Mary and Martha in Luke 10?
- In what ways might you be prioritizing the busyness of life over spending quality time in relationship with God?
- Reflect on any old practices or habits that you need to let go of as you dedicate this year to God. How can embracing a new way of life help you grow and deepen your relationship with Him?
- How does understanding God's desire for relationship with you affect your approach to following Him? What steps can you take to ensure your daily life flows from a place of love rather than obligation?

CHAPTER 8

GOD TIME

It was 2012 and I found myself struggling to connect with God. It was frustrating, unexpected, and I knew a change was needed.

At the time, I was serving on staff as an associate pastor at a church in Alabama. I was helping people get closer to God and leading them to Christ.

From the outside, everything seemed great about that season of my life. But on the inside, I was disconnected. My relationship with God had become stale. I didn't enjoy reading the Bible or spending time in prayer.

That's when 'God Time' began for me.

I've personally learned that giving God a year of your life practically starts with giving Him a piece of your every day.

But not just any piece–the first piece. In doing so, you'll find that everything else falls into place, not because it's less important, but because you've discovered what is most important, just like Mary did!

1 Timothy 4:7–8 instructs, "Have nothing to do with godless myths and old wives' tales; rather, train yourself to be godly. For physical training is of some value, but godliness has value for all things, holding promise for both the present life and the life to come."

Notice it's your responsibility to become godly, not someone else's. It reminds me of the adage, "You can lead a horse to water, but you can't make it drink."

I can give you all the resources. I can put every piece of wisdom and advice possible in this book to help you give God a year of your life. Still, the choice is yours.

Look again at what 1 Timothy 4:7–8 is showing us. The benefits of physical training need no explanation. They have value. But training for godliness? That's something "holding promise for both the present life and the life to come." And that's good news!

In the New American Standard Bible, 1 Timothy 4:8 says to "discipline yourself for the purpose of godliness."

The root word for discipline is disciple, which is exactly what Jesus called us to be. He didn't call us to be only followers. He didn't call us to be observers. He called us to be disciples.

Some of the last words He ever spoke on this earth were, "go and make disciples" (Matt. 28:19).

Only disciples can make other disciples. So, this is a calling straight from our Lord and Savior, to live a life that's being sanctified so we can help others.

That's my goal in this book, especially in this chapter. As I mentioned, giving God a year of your life starts with giving Him a piece of your day.

What does that look like? I discovered in 2012 that it's all about something I lovingly refer to as 'God Time,' defined as nothing more than spending time with God.

There are four keys I want to give you regarding it—

God Time Must Be A Priority

We've already covered priority and putting God first in this book. But in the context of God Time, it means giving God not just any part of your day but the first part.

So, practically, put 'God Time' on your calendar. If you look at mine, you'd find a recurring event for every morning starting at 5:30am labeled, "God Time."

Admittedly, it hasn't always been that way. I haven't always liked getting up early. But as I've set that time aside and guarded it, the benefits have far outweighed the cost of a little less sleep.

Of course, there are opportunities to miss it or make excuses.

Someone might invite you to a morning coffee or perhaps you'd rather go to the gym or have a run than sit in the silence of the morning and pray and read your Bible. I get it. But remember, giving God a year is about relationship. And relationship requires time.

God Time Must Have A Place

We can meet God anywhere. And I want to encourage you to do that! Talk to God in your car. Pray when you're getting your groceries. Sing a worship song in the shower. Meditate on scripture as you do yard work or go on a walk.

But I also want to propose to you there's something powerful about having a special place where you meet with God regularly.

I love how the book of Mark records that Jesus would go by Himself early in the morning, while it was still dark outside, to "a solitary place" (Mk. 1:35).

Your solitary place could be a certain chair in your home. It could be the patio or porch. It could be a spot underneath a tree or a park bench. Perhaps you've heard the term "prayer closet"? Maybe your place could be your closet!

I have an office at home and often have my God time there. No matter where it is, the idea of a place to meet with God isn't for God. It's for you.

It's funny to think about, but God's not up in heaven saying, "Hey, where are we meeting today? I'm not sure where to go!"

He'll meet you wherever you are. But just like you'd let a friend know where you're meeting for coffee or lunch, be intentional and clear about setting a time and space to meet with God.

I remember a song called "In the Secret," written by Andy Park. Some of the lyrics said …

In the secret, in the quiet place

In the stillness You are there,

In the secret, in the quiet hour I wait,

Only for You, 'cause I want to know You more

This beautiful song was about spending time with God, and it's based on Matthew 6:6—

"But when you pray, go into your room, close the door and pray to your Father, who is unseen. Then your Father, who sees what is done in secret, will reward you."

I love how The Message paraphrases that passage.

> "Here's what I want you to do: Find a quiet, secluded place so you won't be tempted to role-play before God. Just be there as simply and honestly as you can manage. The focus will shift from you to God, and you will begin to sense his grace. The world is full of so-called prayer warriors who are prayer-ignorant. They're full of formulas and programs and advice, peddling techniques for getting what you want from God. Don't fall for that nonsense. This is your Father you are dealing with, and he knows better than you what you need. With a God like this loving you, you can pray very simply" (Matt. 6:6–8).

So, make those words personal for you. Remove distractions. Try using a physical Bible to stay fully present, allowing you to focus on God's Word without the interruption of notifications on your phone.

I've had to do this. And even if you're a morning person and find that to be your most productive time, give God ten minutes before you get to work.

Find a place to connect with your Creator and cherish it. Trust me, your day—and your life—will be the better because of it.

God Time Must Have A Plan

One of the most crucial lessons I've learned is that effective God Time requires a plan. Of course, God's agenda comes first, but being prepared is helpful. So, I want to share how I plan to help you develop your own.

Now, I realized that if I wanted to have uninterrupted time with the Lord, I needed to wake up before anyone else in the house.

I love my family, but once my wife and kids are awake, distractions are inevitable, even though they're not intentional. I need to be involved in helping the kids get ready for school, praying over them, and preparing them for the day.

Because of this, I go to bed earlier to wake up earlier. And when I wake up, the first thing I do is make coffee. We jokingly call it Jehovah's Java Juice in our house!

Once my coffee is ready, I begin my prayer time, and I'll pray while I walk around my house.

My favorite way to pray is through a pattern called the Tabernacle Prayer, which I'll go into detail about in a later chapter.

I learned about the Tabernacle Prayer years ago from Pastor Chris Hodges who wrote a fantastic book called *"Pray First."* For now, it's important to understand prayer is simply talking to God.

The Tabernacle Prayer is a pattern that helps guide my conversation with Him.

After prayer, I open my One Year Bible. It's the Bible I mentioned in the previous chapter that I bought when I was sixteen. It's full of highlights, notes, and memories of my journey with God.

Today, for example, I read from Joshua 24, "I gave you land on which you did not toil … (Josh. 24:13)"

I've read this passage before, but today it spoke to me in a new way. It reminded me of how God has blessed me and my family with things we didn't work for—how He has given us more than we could have ever earned on our own.

Sometimes, I don't finish the entire daily reading, and that's okay. The goal isn't to check off a box. It's to engage with God's Word.

How much you read isn't nearly as important as the fact that you ARE reading. It's not just about reading the Bible but letting it read you. On most days, I also take time to journal. I follow a simple method called SOAP.

Scripture—I write down the scripture that stood out to me.

Observation—I observe what it's saying.

Application—I apply the Word to my life.

Prayer—I write out a prayer in response.

Another scripture that stood out to me today was from the same chapter in Joshua, "This stone will be a witness against us" (Josh. 24:27). It reminded me of Jesus' words, "if they keep quiet, the stones will cry out" (Lk. 19:40). I journaled how important it is to praise God and not let anything else take our place in worshiping Him.

Let me encourage you: You don't have to follow my exact pattern. You might think, "Well, you're a pastor. You're paid to do this." But that's not true. God Time isn't about being a pastor. It's about being a Christian.

If you only have fifteen minutes, let me give you a simple plan: Spend five minutes in the Word, five minutes in worship, and five minutes in prayer. But the amount of time isn't as important as the consistency.

- Read the Word, even if it's a few verses.
- Spend a few minutes worshiping God. Maybe sing a song or listen to something on your playlist.
- Finally, spend time in prayer!

God Time Must Be Practiced

Practice doesn't make perfect; it makes permanent.

Think of a professional athlete. Rarely will you find one at the top of their game who doesn't have a coach. Why? Because they need someone to help them practice and remind them of the basics, fundamentals, technique, fitness, and footwork they need to succeed.

The same goes for your favorite singers—they have coaches and practice regularly to maintain and improve their skillset and vocal range.

So why do we sometimes think we can maintain a vibrant, personal relationship with God without regularly meeting with Him? Why do we think we can grow in our faith without consistently setting aside time for Him?

The truth is, we need to put our God Time into practice, just as athletes and performers practice their craft.

If practicing God Time is a challenge for you, my goal in sharing that isn't to make you feel guilty. I want to nudge you forward.

Maybe this is the moment you need to decide, "That's it. I'm ready. Let's do this. I'm giving God a year, so I will give Him the first part of my day."

It may be a challenge at first. It may be a struggle. Even so, keep showing up. Keep practicing. Establish a pattern, a permanent habit of meeting with God.

Remember, God Time is about building a relationship with Him. It's a time to connect, grow, and be strengthened in your faith. Make it a priority, and you'll see your life transformed!

GO ALL IN

- How can you create intentional space in your daily routine to push aside distractions and focus on time with God?
- What are some practical ways you can prioritize God Time each morning? How might this impact the rest of your day and your relationship with God?
- Do you have a specific place where you regularly meet with God? If not, what location in your home or surroundings could become your "solitary place" for God Time?
- How can you actively practice your God Time plan, ensuring that it becomes a permanent part of your life?

CHAPTER 9

WHAT IS THE BIBLE ABOUT?

A few chapters ago, I touched on the beauty of the Smokies near my house growing up. But specifically, my hometown of Sweetwater, TN, was known for two things ...

- A flea market. At its prime, there were over eight HUNDRED indoor dealers of nicknacks, paddy whacks, and anything else you can imagine.
- And something called The Lost Sea.

For nature enthusiasts, The Lost Sea is a must-see attraction. It once claimed the title of "World's Largest Underground Lake." Now, it is simply "America's Largest Underground Lake."

As a native Sweetwater Wildcat (our school's mascot), every student had the opportunity to tour this wonder of the world. The tour included a boat ride on the two-acre underground lake. It was massive. But there was another moment on the tour I'll never forget.

The guide led our group to a massive cavern. I can't emphasize enough just how huge it was, especially to an elementary-age East Tennessee kid.

But then it really got good.

Once we were in the cavern, the guide turned off all the lights to illustrate what complete and utter darkness looked like.

Thankfully, it wasn't dark for long, but the experience left a lasting impression on me. I've never experienced anything like it. We would have been lost if the tour guides hadn't been properly equipped with a flashlight. We'd have had no way to navigate the darkness that surrounded us.

The technical term for people who go into a cave not just for a tour but to explore is "spelunking." It was something I did multiple times with friends as a kid. But it carried its risks.

If you go into a cave without a guide or the proper gear—especially a flashlight—you'll find yourself in a world of trouble. You'll be in a setting you're unfamiliar with, on a path you're unsure of, towards a destination you can't determine without light to provide a path forward.

That's what life is like without the Bible.

The Bible is more than a historical book of stories or a manifesto of morals. It's a guide. It's a flashlight. And as we'll soon see, it's alive.

Growing up, I went to church all the time. And in Sunday school, I learned a lot about the Bible. Or at least I thought I did. I knew all the stories you'd probably recognize even if you didn't attend church every week like me—Adam and Eve, Noah and the ark, David and Goliath, Jonah and the whale, Jesus. etc.

When I was thirteen, God began birthing in my heart a desire to serve in ministry, so I went to Bible College when I graduated high school.

The first day turned my view of the Bible upside down.

My theology professor gave us new students a pop quiz. It was a simple one. Every answer was either true or false. And I was confident when he started.

First, Noah was a woman.

Easy. False. The Bible says he was a man who had three sons and built the ark as God directed him to before the flood.

Hundreds of students were in this class, and everyone replied as I did. "False." Then the Professor said, "Oh, you didn't ask me which Noah. There are two Noahs in the Bible, and one is a woman."

The Professor then says to us, "True or false? There were three wise men."

The students around me were a bit rattled like me but still assured. I mean, there's the old Christmas song, "We Three Kings." Three gifts were given to Jesus—gold, frankincense, and myrrh. Of course there were three wise men.

False.

Again, the Professor explained, "The Bible says the wise men brought three gifts. It doesn't say how many of them there were."

The professor went on to test us with another couple of questions and again, we failed each of them.

I was so frustrated. To an extent, I wanted to give up and go home. But that day taught me I didn't know as much about the Bible as I thought. And what the professor wanted to help us realize was that if you're going to be in ministry and talk about the Bible, then you should probably have a pretty good understanding of it.

When you know what the Bible is and does, and grasp what it's about, you'll set yourself up for success—not only for this challenge to give God a year of your life but every day after.

2 Timothy 3:16–17 reveals, "All Scripture is inspired by God and is useful to teach us what is true and to make us realize what is wrong in our lives. It corrects us when we are wrong and teaches us to do what is right. God uses it to prepare and equip his people to do every good work" (NLT).

The Bible isn't manmade. It comes from God, written through the Holy Spirit while people like you and me held the pens. And what's it for? To help us get closer to God and know what's right and wrong so we can be prepared and equipped for every good work He has for us. Sounds pretty good, right?

The author of Hebrews further says, "For the word of God is alive and active. Sharper than any double-edged sword, it penetrates even to dividing soul and spirit, joints and marrow; it judges the thoughts and attitudes of the heart" (Heb. 4:12).

There's nothing that compares to the words in the Bible. They're given to us by God. They're our playbook, manual, and handbook; a love letter from God to us revealing how we can live, love, and serve Him well.

A theologian, DL Moody, said "the Bible was not given for our information."[8] And in an age where we have smartphones with access to pretty much anything we can think of, we don't need more knowledge. We need life. We need hope. We need transformation. We need God's Word!

Psalm 19 is an amazing passage of scripture that describes this. Multiple verses describe not only facts about the Bible but also benefits with each of them.

"The law of the Lord is perfect, refreshing the soul."

We have laws in America and our communities intended to protect our way of life and keep us safe. Speed limits are an example. But while there are laws in this country we can vote for or legislate to change, God's law—the Word of God—is perfect.

God's Word doesn't need to change. It doesn't need to be altered. It doesn't need to be fixed. And when we lean into it and follow it, it's refreshing for our souls. It doesn't restrict or keep us from having fun; it sets us free!

The passage continues...

---

8 Web. Goodreads, https://www.goodreads.com/quotes/239061-the-bible-was-not-given-for-our-information-but-for. Accessed 5 Dec, 2024.

"⁷The statutes of the Lord are trustworthy, making wise the simple. ⁸The precepts of the Lord are right, giving joy to the heart. The commands of the Lord are radiant, giving light to the eyes. ⁹The fear of the Lord is pure, enduring forever. The decrees of the Lord are firm, and all of them are righteous. ¹⁰They are more precious than gold, than much pure gold; they are sweeter than honey, than honey from the honeycomb. ¹¹By them your servant is warned; in keeping them there is great reward" (Psa. 19:7–11).

Did you notice the characteristics of God's Word? Did you see the benefits?

From wisdom to joy, light, and rewards, the benefits of God's Word are needed, beautiful, and ultimately, endless. So, before we end this chapter about what scripture is, I want to give you three truths to remember.

God's Word instructs us on how to live a holy life

I love what the Psalmist writes in Psalm 32:8, "I will instruct you and teach you in the way you should go; I will counsel you with my loving eye on you."

How does God instruct, teach, and counsel us? While God can speak to our hearts directly, He also uses His Word. And it's so important to have a Bible, whether it's a physical one you hold or an app on your phone. But don't just get a Bible to have it. Read it, think about it, memorize it, and receive God's direction from it.

God doesn't want to leave you high and dry. He doesn't want you to wander in this life unsure of what to do or how to determine the right way to live. He's given you His Word! Start reading it and discover all the truth, promise, hope, and direction He wants to give you through it.

God's word illuminates the dark places of my life

I believe everyone has something in their life that, if removed or transformed, would make life better.

Well, God's Word helps with that! Psalm 119 is the midway point of the Bible. And I don't think it's a coincidence that in the very middle of the Bible, there's a chapter that's all about the Bible. Psalm 119:10–16 says...

> "^{10}I seek you with all my heart; do not let me stray from your commands. ^{11}I have hidden your word in my heart that I might not sin against you. ^{12}Praise be to you, Lord; teach me your decrees. ^{13}With my lips I recount all the laws that come from your mouth. ^{14}I rejoice in following your statutes as one rejoices in great riches. ^{15}I meditate on your precepts and consider your ways. ^{16}I delight in your decrees; I will not neglect your word."

Then verse 105 of that same chapter declares, "Your word is a lamp for my feet, a light on my path."

Just like the story of when I was in the cave and the lights were turned off, we can all feel that way in life. We can find ourselves disoriented, blinded, and overwhelmed. But through God's Word, we have a flashlight.

We have access to something that can illuminate what may be hidden and show us a way out and through every season and struggle life brings.

God's Word indicates when I'm not living a holy life

Think about the dashboard of a car for a moment.

At a glance, you can determine if the car needs gas, if your tire pressure is low, or if there's something wrong with the engine. These things are crucial to the vehicle running smoothly and carrying you safely on the road.

The Bible is similar.

- Just as the check engine light signals that something is wrong with your car's engine, God's Word can highlight when something in your life is off course and needs to be addressed internally.
- The fuel gauge shows how much gas is left before you run out. Similarly, God's Word reveals when you're spiritually running on empty. If you're neglecting God Time, church, or connection with other believers, you can start to feel spiritually drained, like a car running low on fuel.
- Just as ignoring low oil pressure can lead to engine damage, neglecting your spiritual well-being can have severe consequences. God's Word warns you when your "spiritual oil"—your relationship with Him—needs attention.
- If your tires are under-inflated, your car's performance suffers. In the same way, if your faith or trust in God is low, your spiritual walk will be unsteady.
- When the battery light comes on, your car's power is at risk of failing. Similarly, God's Word acts as a warning when you rely on your strength instead of His. If you feel powerless or overwhelmed, get into the Word and be strengthened by God's truth and promises.

I love what Hebrews 12:6–11 says, paraphrased, in The Message—

My dear child, don't shrug off God's discipline, but don't be crushed by it either. It's the child he loves that he disciplines; the child he embraces, he also corrects. God is educating you; that's why you must never drop out. He's treating you as dear children. This trouble you're in isn't punishment; it's training, the normal experience of children. Only irresponsible parents leave children to fend for themselves. Would you prefer an irresponsible God? We respect our own parents for training and not spoiling us, so why not embrace God's training so we can truly live? While we were children, our parents did what seemed best to them. But God is doing what is best for us, training us to live God's holy best. At the time, discipline isn't much fun. It always feels like it's going against the grain. Later, of course, it pays off big-time, for it's the well-trained who find themselves mature in their relationship with God.

Friend, God loves you! He's a good Father. He sacrificed His Son to save you and set you free. When He corrects you through the Word, He doesn't do so with shame or condemnation. He wants to gently reveal when you're missing Him, perhaps stepping outside His will, and lead you back to His best.

It's what His Word—the Bible—is all about. It's an essential aspect of giving Him a year of your life. And as you'll see in the next chapter, it can also protect you when "storms" come, enabling you to live steady and secure.

GO ALL IN

- When was the last time you experienced a moment of spiritual darkness or confusion? How can you seek the light and guidance of God's Word to navigate through it?
- Are there areas where you need to be more intentional about seeking God's Word for truth and to show you the way forward?
- What is one way you will prioritize reading the Bible in the days ahead?

CHAPTER 10

A FIRM FOUNDATION

East Tennessee isn't known for its storms.

North Texas is.

Here in Wichita Falls, tornado watches and warnings come with the territory. People here, for the most part, get used to them.

That being said, I don't know anyone who'd want to hunker down for a tornado in a home that doesn't have a firm foundation. When there's any possibility of a swirling vortex of a hundred-mile-per-hour wind, you recognize the danger and take the appropriate precautions.

While Jesus didn't mention Texas or tornadoes in His ministry, He did talk about storms. He spoke of the wind and waves we can face in life. I'm sure you're as familiar with them as I am. They can look like …

- Marital strife
- Financial debt
- The loss of a loved one
- Struggles at work

When storms like those happen, it's essential your house—your life—isn't built on something shaky but steady.

You need to build on the Word of God.

In Matthew 7:24–27, Jesus talked about two men who built their own houses—one on a rock, the other on sand.

The one who built on the rock put Jesus' words into practice. The other one didn't. And when the storms came, when the winds blew, the "rock" house stood firm. The "sand" one fell apart.

You see, in the previous chapter, we learned what the Bible is about. Now, we need to understand what happens when we put it into practice, as well as the obstacles that may come along the way.

My Bible college professor didn't orchestrate that pop quiz I told you about merely to expose his students' lack of knowledge. He wanted to awaken us to the reality that the Bible is so much more than we had previously thought it was.

The Bible generates life. The Word of God creates faith. It produces a change in us. It's a weapon against evil in this world. It can't be a book we read occasionally. It needs to be an integral part of daily life.

Let me take you to Genesis momentarily because doubting God's Word isn't new. It happened from the very beginning of recorded history and time.

In Genesis 1 and 2, we see God place Adam and Eve in the Garden of Eden, a paradise where they could enjoy everything except one tree—the Tree of the Knowledge of Good and Evil.

God's command was clear: "You are free to eat from any tree in the garden; but you must not eat from the tree of the knowledge of good and evil, for when you eat from it you will certainly die" (Gen. 2:16-17).

Satan, in the form of a serpent, slithered into the garden. Approaching Eve, he whispered, "Did God really say, 'You must not eat from any tree in the garden?'" (Gen. 3:1). Eve replied that they could eat from any tree except the one in the middle of the garden for they would die if they did" (Gen. 3:2).

Then Satan, crafty and cunning, challenged God's word. "'You will not certainly die,' the serpent said to the woman. 'For God knows that when you eat from it your eyes will be opened, and you will be like God, knowing good and evil'" (Gen. 3:4–5).

Tempted by the serpent's words, Eve took the fruit, ate it, and gave some to Adam, who also ate (Gen. 3:6). At that moment, sin and death entered the world.

Satan hates the Word of God. He doesn't want you to just question it. He wants you to doubt and reject it. He'll come to you and whisper, "Did God really say that? Do you think He means it? That's not God."

Just as Satan deceived Adam and Eve, he continues to tempt and try to deceive us today. But remember, God's Word is truth, and standing firm on it is our best defense against the enemy's lies.

Jesus shows us this. In Matthew 4, Jesus is led by the Holy Spirit into the wilderness for forty days to fast, pray, and prepare for the following three years of ministry.

Of course, as He fasts, He becomes hungry. And that's when Satan attacks.

> [3]The tempter came to him and said, "If you are the Son of God, tell these stones to become bread." [4]Jesus answered, "It is written: 'Man shall not live on bread alone, but on every word that comes from the mouth of God.' [5]Then the devil took him to the holy city and had him stand on the highest point of the temple. [6]'If you are the Son of God,' he said, "throw yourself down. For it is written: 'He will command his angels concerning you, and they will lift you up in their hands, so that you will not strike your foot against a stone.' [7]Jesus answered him, 'It is also written: 'Do not put the Lord your God to the test.' [8]Again, the devil took him to a very high mountain and showed him all the kingdoms of the world and their splendor. [9]'All this I will give you,' he said, 'if you will bow down and worship me.' [10]Jesus said to him, 'Away from me, Satan! For it is written: 'Worship the Lord your God, and serve him only.' [11]Then the devil left him, and angels came and attended him" (Matt. 4:3–11).

Isn't that incredible? Three times, Satan challenged God's Word. Three times, Jesus met that challenge with what? God's Word!

Current culture might cancel the Bible. In some countries, you can even be arrested for reading it. Nevertheless, make up your mind today that "as for me and my house, we will serve the Lord (Josh. 24:15)."

Trust me, the Bible is the one thing you can count on and stand on in a world where everything else is uncertain and changing.

As you make the Bible your foundation, I have three declarations I want to give you.

Declaration 1:
"I will absorb the Bible."

Reading it once a week isn't enough. Skimming it for highlights won't satisfy. Interestingly, some research indicates that reading the Bible once or twice a week has little to no effect, while reading it four times per week brings a wealth of benefits. It's called "The Power of 4."[9]

Jesus tells us, "Remain in me, as I also remain in you. No branch can bear fruit by itself; it must remain in the vine. Neither can you bear fruit unless you remain in me. I am the vine; you are the branches. If you remain in me and I in you, you will bear much fruit; apart from me you can do nothing" (Jn. 15:4–5).

Read the Word. Love it. Ingest it. Let it take root in your life, and your fruit—your behavior—will be full of the hope and love of Jesus.

---

9   Web. Center for Bible Engagement, https://www.centerforbibleengagement.org/research. Accessed 5 Dec, 2024.

Declaration 2:
"I will accept God's word as the final authority in my life."

For a long time in the American judicial system, it was required for anyone testifying in a court of law to put their hand on a Bible and swear to tell the truth.

As a culture, we've gotten away from that. In our lives, we can stray from it. But today, I want to encourage you to commit that regardless of whether you agree with the Bible, you'll make it the final authority in your life. And here's the promise:

> "Keep this Book of the Law always on your lips; meditate on it day and night, so that you may be careful to do everything written in it. Then you will be prosperous and successful" (Josh. 1:8).

Declaration 3:
"I will apply the Bible as absolute truth."

This declaration doesn't mean the Bible becomes a measuring stick you use to judge and condemn others.

Unfortunately, there are Christians and churches who misrepresent God's grace and espouse ridicule and hate. This breaks my heart because, as we've already learned, it was for love God sacrificed His son to save us (Jn. 3:16).

At my church, City Hope, in my life, and in yours, it's my prayer we would model and express a life overflowing with that love.

1 Corinthians 13:1–3 says, "[1]If I speak in the tongues of men or of angels, but do not have love, I am only a resounding gong or a clanging cymbal. [2]If I have the gift of prophecy and can fathom all mysteries and all knowledge, and if I have a faith that can move mountains, but do not have love, I am nothing. [3]If I give all I possess to the poor

and give over my body to hardship that I may boast, but do not have love, I gain nothing."

Then verse 13 ends with this powerful statement, "And now these three remain: faith, hope and love. But the greatest of these is love."

Make no mistake, the Bible is a book of love. It isn't restrictive. It's freeing. It isn't hateful. It's hopeful. It isn't doom and gloom but life and peace.

Still, the Bible isn't something you bend to fit your lifestyle. It stands on its own. It's authoritative. It's the word of truth. It isn't a book of tales from the past. It's full of revelation for your present and future.

Understanding this, we can be empowered to share this good news with the world, not with a heart of hatred but with a spirit overflowing with love. We can be committed to the truth yet still gracious and compassionate.

It's the foundation on which God wants us to build our lives. And here's the remarkable thing; when you live by God's Word, love it, and apply it to your life, the Bible makes a promise to us. It says that you will flourish!

> "¹Blessed is the one who does not walk in step with the wicked or stand in the way that sinners take or sit in the company of mockers, ²but whose delight is in the law of the Lord, and who meditates on his law day and night. ³That person is like a tree planted by streams of water, which yields its fruit in season and whose leaf does not wither-whatever they do prospers" (Psa. 1:1–3).

God's desire for you is that you would fall in love with His Word and flourish in every area of your life.

There's nothing like the Bible and all the hope, truth, life, and love it brings. It provides us with stories and parables we can learn from. It equips us to follow God. And, as we'll discover in the next chapter, it introduces us to an amazing person who ultimately makes this Christian life possible.

GO ALL IN

- How can you practically absorb and apply the Bible daily?
- How do you respond when cultural norms or societal pressures contradict the teachings of the Bible? Are you tempted to compromise?
- When faced with life's storms—whether in relationships, finances, or personal struggles—how can you ensure your response is rooted in the truth and authority of God's Word?

CHAPTER 11

WHO IS THE HOLY SPIRIT?

I was in my second year of Bible college, attending a class called "Life of Christ."

One day, we were given an assignment: Choose a miracle Jesus did, replicate it, then write a paper about our experience.

Well, Jesus did some big miracles.

- He turned water into wine (Jn. 2:1–11).
- He healed the sick (Matt. 8:14–17).
- He restored the lame to walk (Jn. 5:1–15).
- He brought sight to the blind (Jn. 9:1–12).
- He stopped a storm (Mark 4:35–41).
- He raised the dead to life (Jn. 11:38–44).

Being an achiever at heart, I was ready to go all in. I remember thinking, *Should I find a funeral home and lay hands on a body? Should I look for someone in a wheelchair?*

The Bible College was in Florida, and it just so happened that a tropical storm was about to make landfall. So, I decided to go and tell the wind and waves to be still, just like Jesus did!

Before I tell you my experience, let's read what happened to Jesus in Mark 4:35–41.

> [35]That day when evening came, he said to his disciples, 'Let us go over to the other side.' [36]Leaving the crowd behind, they took him along, just as he was, in the boat. There were also other boats with him. [37]A furious squall came up, and the waves

broke over the boat, so that it was nearly swamped. ³⁸Jesus was in the stern, sleeping on a cushion. The disciples woke him and said to him, 'Teacher, don't you care if we drown?' ³⁹He got up, rebuked the wind and said to the waves, 'Quiet! Be still!' Then the wind died down and it was completely calm. ⁴⁰He said to his disciples, 'Why are you so afraid? Do you still have no faith?' ⁴¹They were terrified and asked each other, 'Who is this? Even the wind and the waves obey him!'

I had never been through a tropical storm. I didn't know what to expect. I wore a windbreaker and shorts, got in my Nissan Xterra, and drove to Perdido Key—my favorite beach spot.

When I arrived at the public beach area, I walked to the top of some dunes by the ocean. The winds were fierce around me, pelting me with sand. It felt like someone was sandblasting my legs. Bad call on wearing shorts.

The storm was raging. But just like Jesus, I stood and declared, "Peace! Be still, in Jesus' name!"

As God as my witness, you will not believe what happened next.

Nothing.

And in case you were wondering, other people were around me.

It was a tropical storm, not a hurricane so while the wind was strong, people didn't need to hole up in their homes. People wanted to see the storm. And there I was, believing I could cancel that storm in Jesus' name!

Yet nothing happened.

I gave it three solid attempts. Then I drove home and wrote a paper about it!

Now, I know what you're thinking: Ben, did you really think you could stop a storm? Genuinely, yes! Here's why: Jesus said in John 14:12, "Very truly I tell you, whoever believes in me will do the works I have been doing, and they will do even greater things than these…"

WHO IS THE HOLY SPIRIT?

Jesus didn't just say that. He meant it. Yet our human tendency is to think God can only do what makes sense in our brain. We box Him in according to what we believe is possible. But what if God is bigger than that?

Many people want to serve God on an intellectual level. They want to understand His nature, decipher His character, and have lectures about who He is and what He does. And while none of that is wrong in and of itself, we ultimately need more than lectures and intellect. We need more than understanding to see freedom. We need more than a lecture to bring healing. We need the power and presence of God to fill our hearts and minds, break down walls, heal the sick, and bring hope to the hopeless.

God is still in the miracle-working business. If you doubt that, I understand. I have too. But I know miracles can still happen because of a person Jesus came to this earth to introduce us to: The Holy Spirit.

The Holy Spirit isn't some force or ghost (though you may have heard Him referred to as the Holy Ghost).

He's a person. He's not weird. He is God. He's someone who can counsel you, teach you, guide you, and help you every day. He can be and wants to be your best friend!

Here are just a few of the things the Bible says about Him ...

"But the Advocate, the Holy Spirit, whom the Father will send in my name, will teach you all things and will remind you of everything I have said to you" (Jn. 14:26).

"For John baptized with water, but in a few days you will be baptized with the Holy Spirit" (Acts 1:5).

"...our gospel came to you not simply with words but also with power, with the Holy Spirit and deep conviction"(1 Thess. 1:5).

"And hope does not put us to shame, because God's love has been poured out into our hearts through the Holy Spirit, who has been given to us" (Rom. 5:5).

"I will give you a new heart and put a new spirit in you; I will remove from you your heart of stone and give you a heart of flesh. And I will put my Spirit in you and move you to follow my decrees and be careful to keep my laws" (Ez. 36:26–27).

The Holy Spirit is a BIG deal. He's omnipresent, meaning He will always be with you. He reveals the Bible. He helps you share your faith with others. He convicts you of sin. He guides you through life.

The Bible also refers to Him as the "Spirit of God," and you can find Him in the very first chapter. Genesis 1:2 tells us, "Now the earth was formless and empty, darkness was over the surface of the deep, and the Spirit of God was hovering over the waters."

There are two takeaways for us in this scripture.

First, we can see that the Holy Spirit was present from the beginning of recorded time. He was in the middle of the formless, empty darkness that became God's creation. I love that because it serves as a potent reminder that even in our darkest moments, when we feel empty and void of hope, the Holy Spirit is there!

Second, Genesis was originally written in Hebrew, and the Hebrew word for Spirit is *rûwach*.[10] This word means wind, breath, and a sensible (or even violent) exhalation.

The New Testament was written in Greek but the word for Spirit is translated similarly. The word is *pneuma*, meaning a current of air, blast of breath, or breeze.[11]

---

10   H7307 - rûaḥ - Strong's Hebrew Lexicon (niv)." Blue Letter Bible. Web. <https://www.blueletterbible.org/lexicon/h7307/kjv/wlc/0-1/>. Accessed 5 Dec, 2024.

11   G4151 - pneuma - Strong's Greek Lexicon (niv)." Blue Letter Bible. Web. <https://www.blueletterbible.org/lexicon/g4151/kjv/tr/0-1/>. Accessed 5 Dec, 2024.

So, what's the Holy Spirit like? Well, He's not *like* breath. He *is* breath. He's wind in your sails. He's life in your lungs.

You and I are both familiar with breath and wind. We breathe oxygen. It's how we live. We feel the wind. It's part of our experience on earth. But I want to focus on a couple of characteristics of wind that can help us discover more about who the Holy is. Here's the first —

The Holy Spirit goes unseen.

When it's windy outside, you don't see the wind. You might notice leaves or other debris flying in the air. You experience the wind, but when it comes to the wind in and of itself, it goes unseen.

Like the wind, you can feel the Holy Spirit but can't see Him.

At City Hope Church, I love hearing stories from people who've attended our services and talked about how amazing it was or how great it felt. But they might as well have been talking about the wind! What they were experiencing wasn't just incredible music, a helpful teaching, or friendly people. They were experiencing the presence and power of the Holy Spirit.

Now, I understand if the fact you can't see the Holy Spirit makes you uncomfortable.

It's said that "seeing is believing," but the reality is that "seeing" doesn't take faith. It takes faith to believe in the Holy Spirit. It takes faith to recognize Him as a person and realize His presence is in and around you—just like it takes faith to believe in God. Nevertheless, I want you to know that Jesus is so excited and proud of you when you choose to believe!

In John 20, Jesus appears to His disciples soon after He was raised from the dead. The disciples were all gathered in a house together. Scripture is detailed enough to point out the door was locked. Yet, suddenly, Jesus appears and absolutely freaks them out! We know this because His first words are, "Peace be with you!" (Jn. 20:19).

"20 After he said this, he showed them his hands and side. The disciples were overjoyed when they saw the Lord. 21 Again Jesus said, 'Peace be with you! As the Father has sent me, I am sending you.' 22 And with that he breathed on them and said, 'Receive the Holy Spirit'" (Jn. 20:20–22).

There was one disciple who wasn't there—Thomas. The other disciples told him what happened, but he said, "Unless I see the nail marks in his hands and put my finger where the nails were, and put my hand into his side, I will not believe" (Jn. 20:25).

A week later, they were in a room together again, and Jesus showed up. This time, Thomas was there.

"[27]Then he said to Thomas, 'Put your finger here; see my hands. Reach out your hand and put it into my side. Stop doubting and believe.' [28]Thomas said to him, 'My Lord and my God!' [29]Then Jesus told him, 'Because you have seen me, you have believed; blessed are those who have not seen and yet have believed'" (Jn. 20:27–29).

So, what's the lesson for us? Just because you can't see the Holy Spirit doesn't mean He's not working and moving. Even though He goes unseen, I want to encourage you to believe in Him.

The Holy Spirit is unpredictable.

While meteorology can help us determine when wind direction and speed may change, it's still out of our control. It's not 100% predictable.

The same is true for the Holy Spirit. But this doesn't mean He only works in last-minute or spontaneous moments.

I know some folks who won't plan because they feel they're planning the Holy Spirit out of their life. I have a different perspective. I believe the Holy Spirit can speak to us about something days, weeks, months, even years in advance. And yet, He also reserves the right to change His mind.

Many denominations form their entire theology of the Holy Spirit around one person's experience. But remember, the Holy Spirit is unpredictable. Check out what Jesus said to a man named Nicodemus about this very thing—

"The wind blows wherever it pleases. You hear its sound, but you cannot tell where it comes from or where it is going. So it is with everyone born of the Spirit" (Jn. 3:8).

In other words, if you want to be close to God, there's something you'll need to get used to, and that's the unpredictable nature of the Holy Spirit.

Thankfully, however, there are a few more characteristics of the Holy Spirit you can recognize Him by.

He counsels

The Holy Spirit wants to give you wisdom and knowledge to make decisions that move you forward in God's best for your life.

He convicts

In John 16:8, Jesus talks about how the Holy Spirit will convict us of sin and God's righteousness. In other words, the Holy Spirit will help us know when we've taken a wrong turn or made a mistake, not to shame us but to remind us of our righteous identity in Christ!

He completes

I've already mentioned this but it bears repeating: Giving God a year isn't possible without the Holy Spirit. We will experience a "completeness" in our lives with Him and only with Him.

Remember, the Holy Spirit is a person, but He isn't subject to our plans. He's breath. He's life. He's like the wind, but He isn't destructive.

He's powerful, and as we'll see in the next chapter, He's empowering without being a force to be feared.

The Holy Spirit is truly amazing! After salvation, nothing can change your life more than knowing Him. And in the next chapter, I'll share more with you about what He does and why inviting Him to have His way within you is critical to giving God a year of your life.

GO ALL IN

- Do you ever find yourself trying to fit God into what you think is possible? How can you expand your faith to believe in God's ability to do more than you can imagine?
- How has this chapter challenged or changed your understanding of who the Holy Spirit is?
- In what ways have you experienced the presence of the Holy Spirit in your life? How does recognizing Him as a person, rather than a mere "force," change how you relate to Him?

CHAPTER 12

AN EMPOWERED LIFE

A person's final words are often noteworthy. They can be humorous, tragic, or impactful.

Leonardo da Vinci, who painted the Mona Lisa purportedly said, "I have offended God and mankind because my work didn't reach the quality it should have."[12]

Bob Marley, the Jamaican singer and songwriter, said, "Money can't buy life."[13]

Do you know what Jesus said? I'm not referring to Jesus' last words on the cross. Those words are equally impactful, but I want to focus on what He said before He ascended to heaven after His resurrection. He commanded the disciples to do one last thing …

> "Do not leave Jerusalem, but wait for the gift my Father promised, which you have heard me speak about. For John baptized with water, but in a few days you will be baptized with the Holy Spirit" (Acts 1:4–5).

Why was Jesus so adamant about the Holy Spirit? After all, this is the Son of God we're talking about. His disciples had spent three years with Him. Almost every minute of the day and night, they were near Him, watching Him, listening to Him, discovering what it meant to give God not just a year of their life but all of it.

---

12   "Leonardo da Vinci Quotes." BrainyQuote.com. BrainyMedia Inc, 2024. https://www.brainyquote.com/quotes/leonardo_da_vinci_154283. Accessed 5 Dec, 2024.

13   "Bob Marley Quotes." BrainyQuote.com. BrainyMedia Inc, 2024. https://www.brainyquote.com/quotes/bob_marley_578989 Accessed 5 Dec, 2024.

Yet, Jesus told them that wasn't enough. They needed the Holy Spirit.

You see, in the previous chapter, we learned about who the Holy Spirit is. We discovered what He's like. Now, I want to encourage you with what your life will look like when you experience what He does.

Wouldn't you love having someone in your life who loves you, is always with you, and desires to help you? I do!

Jesus said in Acts 1:8, "But you will receive power when the Holy Spirit comes on you…"

That word power is the Greek word *dynamis*.[14] It isn't a license to do whatever you want. It's a "miraculous power" to follow God.

Furthermore, Jesus refers to the Holy Spirit in John 14:16 as *paraklētos* in Greek.[15] This word is so fascinating. It means intercessor, advocate, or comforter. Clearly, the Holy Spirit's deepest desire is to help you!

Consider Peter and the transformation that happened in his life after he received the gift of the Holy Spirit.

He was the same man who denied Jesus three times. Then, after Jesus died, he hid and returned to his old fishing life. Yet, fifty days later, he preached the gospel to a huge crowd—three thousand of whom were saved.

What happened? What made the difference? What turned his cowardice into confidence? The Holy Spirit!

> "[1]When the day of Pentecost came, they were all together in one place. [2]Suddenly a sound like the blowing of a violent wind came from heaven and filled the whole house where they were sitting. [3]They saw what seemed to be tongues

---

14   G1411 - dynamis - Strong's Greek Lexicon (kjv)." Blue Letter Bible. Web. <https://www.blueletterbible.org/lexicon/g1411/kjv/tr/0-1/>. Accessed 5 Dec, 2024.

15   G3875 - paraklētos - Strong's Greek Lexicon (kjv)." Blue Letter Bible. Web.

of fire that separated and came to rest on each of them. ⁴All of them were filled with the Holy Spirit and began to speak in other tongues as the Spirit enabled them" (Acts 2:1–4).

Peter may have been afraid. Perhaps he was nervous to receive into his life a person and presence he couldn't control. Nevertheless, Peter went all in. He gave God his life. He trusted the Holy Spirit, and everything changed in and through him for the better.

You're doing the same. You're reading this book, you've made Jesus your Lord and Savior, and taken on the challenge of giving God a year of your life.

In the same way you've gone all in on reading the Bible, going to church, and prioritizing your relationship with God, it's time to go all in with the Holy Spirit.

In Ezekiel 47:3–5, there's an amazing prophetic passage that illustrates this. It begins—

> "³As the man went eastward with a measuring line in his hand, he measured off a thousand cubits and then led me through water that was ankle-deep."

The first part of this prophecy describes salvation. It's the first step into the living water—abundant life—Jesus offers us.

> "⁴He measured off another thousand cubits and led me through water that was knee-deep. He measured off another thousand and led me through water that was up to the waist."

Waist deep water is where you begin to feel the wind, the current, the presence of the Holy Spirit. However, at this point, you're keeping Him at arm's length. You've got your heels in and bracing against giving His flow total control.

But look at what happens when you go deeper—

> "⁵He measured off another thousand, but now it was a river that I could not cross, because the water had risen and was deep enough to swim in—a river that no one could cross."

This is the kind of life God wants for us—where we're in over our heads and out of our control so we can be led and empowered by the Holy Spirit, giving Him control. And here are the results …

"Swarms of living creatures will live wherever the river flows. There will be large numbers of fish, because this water flows there and makes the salt water fresh; so where the river flows everything will live… Fruit trees of all kinds will grow on both banks of the river. Their leaves will not wither, nor will their fruit fail. Every month they will bear fruit, because the water from the sanctuary flows to them. Their fruit will serve for food and their leaves for healing" (Ezek. 47:9,12).

Where are you in that prophetic picture? How deep have you stepped into the river?

Wherever you are now, let me encourage you to take a step forward. 1 Corinthians 4:20 says that the Kingdom of God isn't a lot of talk; it's living by God's power.

For many, the Kingdom, tragically, is talk. There's no *dynamis*, no empowerment to follow God's Word and live for Him.

We get saved and think salvation marks the beginning and end of our journey with God. Meanwhile, He has so much more for us! While salvation secures our eternity in heaven, the Holy Spirit gives us the empowerment we need on earth.

Galatians 5:22-23 gives us an even clearer picture of what the Holy Spirit brings. It reads, "But the fruit (the effects) of the Spirit is love, joy, peace, forbearance, kindness, goodness, faithfulness, gentleness and self-control." Sounds pretty good, right?

We've already seen the Holy Spirit's impact on someone like Peter. But two more stories in the New Testament further illustrate what the Holy Spirit does.

"[1]While Apollos was at Corinth, Paul took the road through the interior and arrived at Ephesus. There he found some disciples and [2]asked them, 'Did you receive the Holy

Spirit when you believed?' They answered, 'No, we have not even heard that there is a Holy Spirit.' ³So Paul asked, 'Then what baptism did you receive?' 'John's baptism,' they replied. ⁴Paul said, 'John's baptism was a baptism of repentance. He told the people to believe in the one coming after him, that is, in Jesus.' ⁵On hearing this, they were baptized in the name of the Lord Jesus. ⁶When Paul placed his hands on them, the Holy Spirit came on them, and they spoke in tongues and prophesied" (Acts 19:1–6).

"⁵Philip went down to a city in Samaria and proclaimed the Christ there… ¹²But when they believed Philip as he preached the good news of the kingdom of God and the name of Jesus Christ, they were baptized, both men and women … ¹⁴When the apostles in Jerusalem heard that Samaria had accepted the word of God, they sent Peter and John to them. ¹⁵When they arrived, they prayed for them that they might receive the Holy Spirit, ¹⁶because the Holy Spirit had not yet come upon any of them; they had simply been baptized into the name of the Lord Jesus. ¹⁷Then Peter and John placed their hands on them, and they received the Holy Spirit" (Acts 8:5, 12, 14–17).

Two different experiences. Two separate occasions of apostles and disciples encountering Christians who were saved yet hadn't received the gift of the Holy Spirit. And in both instances, the next step for these believers couldn't have been clearer—receive the Holy Spirit!

Ephesians 4:30 in The Message implores us, "Don't grieve God. Don't break his heart. His Holy Spirit, moving and breathing in you, is the most intimate part of your life, making you fit for himself. Don't take such a gift for granted."

Friend, the good things God has for you are on the other side of you receiving the gift of the Holy Spirit.

"Every good and perfect gift is from above, coming down from the Father of the heavenly lights, who does not change like shifting shadows (James 1:17)."

God wants to give us good gifts. He wants to provide us with more, but we limit our capacity for that more when we keep the Holy Spirit at arm's length.

In Acts 2:38–39, Peter—the same Peter who the Holy Spirit transformed—encouraged others, "Repent and be baptized, every one of you, in the name of Jesus Christ for the forgiveness of your sins. And you will receive the gift of the Holy Spirit. The promise is for you and your children and for all who are far off—for all whom the Lord our God will call."

Right now, God is calling you. He's drawing you into a deeper, more fulfilling, more wonderful, more powerful relationship with Him through the person and presence of the Holy Spirit.

In the next chapter, we'll dive deep into the topic of prayer, but right now, I invite you to pray with me. Tell God, "If You have it, I want it."

There's no room for comfort or complacency in those words. But there is breakthrough. There is transformation. There is blessing on the other side of that decision to go "all in."

Today, be filled with the Holy Spirit. As the Apostle Paul encouraged the church of Corinthians, "May the amazing grace of Jesus, the extravagant love of God, and the intimate friendship of the Holy Spirit, be with you" (2 Cor. 13:14, MSG).

GO ALL IN

- Look back on your life for a moment. Are there seasons and situations when you could have relied upon the Holy Spirit's help?
- When you face moments of fear or uncertainty, like Peter before Pentecost, how can you turn to the Holy Spirit for boldness and confidence instead of retreating to what's familiar?
- Are there areas in your faith where you feel ankle-deep or waist-deep, yet are still hesitant to go all in with the Holy Spirit? What's keeping you from taking that next step?

CHAPTER 13

MAKING PRAYER PERSONAL

It was 2007 and I was on staff at Daystar Church in Cullman, Alabama. Another pastor was there who was about to start a church. I was talking to him about his new journey of church planting, in a parking lot of all places, and I'll never forget when he said, "Maybe Daystar will help you start a church one day."

Something lit up in my heart when he said that. I knew it was God calling me. At the same time, however, I was very aware I had no idea how to start a church!

Fast forward to 2017, everything in my life seemed perfect. My wife and I had just bought a new house in a beautiful neighborhood. Our kids were students at the best school in the area. Daystar Church was thriving. Everything was perfect on paper. And yet, on the inside, I was miserable. Something was missing.

In the midst of that sweet yet confusing season, I talked to a friend who served as a life coach for me. He could tell that something was off.

Randomly, he asked me, "Ben, how old are you?"

"Thirty-five," I told him.

"Sounds like the ripe age of a church planter."

Immediately, the dream came back to life.

I talked to my pastor at Daystar Church—who is still my pastor to this day. He gave my wife and me his blessing and we dedicated the following months to prayer.

As we prayed, God spoke to us, guided us, and provided for us. Long story short, over six hundred people eventually showed up for our first service at City Hope Church in Wichita Falls, TX.

It was a dream come true—a dream that continues to this day. But it was a dream conceived and birthed in prayer.

It's why, as a church, we start each year with twenty-one days of fasting and prayer. We don't want to make one decision, take one action, or put one foot forward without praying about it first.

Ephesians 6:18 says, "And pray in the Spirit (the Holy Spirit!) on all occasions with all kinds of prayers and requests."

I've touched on prayer in some of the earlier chapters but let me reiterate that prayer is nothing more than talking to God. It's that simple and, honestly, that easy! Hebrews 4:16 encourages us, "Let us then approach God's throne of grace with confidence, so that we may receive mercy and find grace to help us in our time of need."

How can we approach God's throne? Through prayer! And according to Ephesians 6:18, we can make different types of prayers and requests for various situations.

For example, there is the Lord's Prayer that Jesus prayed in Matthew 6:9-13. This prayer serves as a model for approaching God with reverence, seeking His will, asking for daily needs, confessing sins, and furthering His Kingdom.

There's Hannah's prayer of petition in 1 Samuel 1. For years, she fervently asked God for a child. She would cry out to God so passionately that people thought she was drunk! Yet her humility, trust, and faith in God serve as powerful examples. What's more, God answered her prayers!

In 1 Kings 8:22-53, King Solomon's temple dedication is a model for prayer on behalf of others. He asks for God's blessing, forgiveness, and guidance for the people of Israel.

Another is "the Tabernacle Prayer," which I want to hone in on for a moment.

Pastor Chris Hodges from Church of the Highlands has spoken on this prayer extensively, and I've learned much from him. His book, *Pray First*, would be a great resource for you to learn even more about prayer in the days ahead!

Now, in Exodus 25:9, God tells Moses and the Israelites, "Make this tabernacle and all its furnishings exactly like the pattern I will show you."

At that time, God lived in places built by human hands. And the specifications He gave them for this tabernacle were incredibly precise. Seven stations were to be set up within it, and the priests had to pass through each one to experience God's presence.

Thankfully, this protocol is no longer required. Because of Jesus, the veil that separated priests from the intensity of God's presence has been torn. We can approach Him boldly because He now lives within us!

However, the Tabernacle is still something we can learn from. The seven stations become steps to guide us in prayer.

#1
The Outer Court
THANKSGIVING AND PRAISE

"Enter his gates with thanksgiving and his courts with praise; give thanks to him and praise his name" (Psa. 100:4).

Similar to how Jesus begins the Lord's Prayer, start by praising God and giving thanks for the good things He's done. After decades of following God, I can't emphasize enough how powerful it is to worship God and thank Him for His salvation, redemption, healing, and blessings.

#2
The Brazen Alter
THE CROSS OF JESUS

"'He himself bore our sins' in his body on the cross, so that we might die to sins and live for righteousness...' (1 Pet. 2:24).

Under the old covenant, everyone who sinned had to present God with a sacrifice to atone for them. But because of Jesus and the cross, He's paid the price for our sins once and for all. Remembering this and the many benefits His finished work has made possible on our behalf is powerful to include in your prayers.

#3
The Laver
CLEANSING AND PREPARING

"But if we walk in the light, as he is in the light, we have fellowship with one another, and the blood of Jesus, his Son, purifies us from all sin" (1 John 1:7).

The laver was a bowl of water to wash and be made clean with. While physical cleanliness is no requirement to enter God's presence today (though probably appreciated by those around you!), spend time praying for God to purify your heart and motives.

Personally, I'll often spend more time on this part of the Tabernacle Prayer than any other. I'll pray Romans 12:1–2, "Therefore, I urge you, brothers and sisters, in view of God's mercy, to offer your bodies as a living sacrifice, holy and pleasing to God—this is your true and proper worship. Do not conform to the pattern of this world, but be transformed by the renewing of your mind. Then you will be able to test and approve what God's will is—his good, pleasing and perfect will."

The word conform is the Greek word *syschēmatizō*, pronounced soos-khay-mat-id'-zo. It means to "conform one's self to another's pattern."[16] In other words, while the world has its way of doing things, God has His.

Then there's the word transformed which in Greek is *metamorphoō*. This is where we get our word "metamorphosis." It means "to change into another form."[17]

This scripture shows us how to become like Christ, and the key is to spend time with Him, which is why this chapter is so timely. We've already covered "God time" and the importance of God's Word and prayer. Now we need to understand the fruit of spending time with Him, and that's becoming like Him through the practice of prayer.

I'll pray, "Lord, I commit today to live for You and You alone. I won't allow myself to lust after people, possessions, and power."

Those three words actually align with 1 John 2:16 when it says, "For everything in the world—the lust of the flesh, the lust of the eyes, and the pride of life—comes not from the Father but from the world."

I'll also pray, "God, let my ears hear Your voice. Let my words bless and not curse. Help me encourage others and serve You in all I do." Then I'll turn to the topic of transformation and say, "Lord, I give You my mind today. Transform my thoughts. Remind me of Your truth when I'm struggling or in need." I reflect on the peace God promises when I think about what is true, right, pure, lovely, and praiseworthy according to Philippians 4:8.

---

16   G4964 - syschēmatizō - Strong's Greek Lexicon (kjv)." Blue Letter Bible. Web. <https://www.blueletterbible.org/lexicon/g4964/kjv/tr/0-1/>. Accessed 5 Dec, 2024.

17   G3339 - metamorphoō - Strong's Greek Lexicon (kjv)." Blue Letter Bible. Web. <https://www.blueletterbible.org/lexicon/g3339/kjv/tr/0-1/>. 5 Dec, 2024.

I encourage you to make each step of the Tabernacle Prayer personal to you.

#4
The Candlestick
THE HOLY SPIRIT

"He (Jesus) will baptize you with the Holy Spirit and fire" (Matt. 3:11).

The candlestick was golden and seven-branched. Each candle had a different meaning but the fire from each one stood for the Spirit of God—the Holy Spirit! In this step, pray for more of the Holy Spirit's presence in your life. Ask Him again to have His way in and through you each day.

#5
The Table of Shrewbread
THE WORD OF GOD

"Keep this Book of the Law always on your lips; meditate on it day and night, so that you may be careful to do everything written in it. Then you will be prosperous and successful" (Josh. 1:8).

The table of shewbread had twelve loaves of bread, representing the importance of reading God's Word. When the enemy tempted Jesus in the desert, His first response was, "Man shall not live by bread alone but every word that proceeds from the mouth of God" (see Matt 4:4). In prayer, we can heed that call and meditate on God's Word.

#6
The Altar of Incense
WORSHIP

"God is spirit, and his worshipers must worship in the Spirit and in truth" (Jn. 4:24).

As I already mentioned, the "Holy of Holies" was where God's presence dwelt within the Tabernacle. But at its entrance stood a small altar of burning incense. This altar represents worship; at its heart, worship expresses love and adoration to God—something that happens when we pray.

#7
The Ark of the Covenant
INTERCESSION

"I urge, then, first of all, that requests, prayers, intercession and thanksgiving be made for everyone—for kings and all those in authority, that we may live peaceful and quiet lives in all godliness and holiness. This is good, and pleases God our Savior, who wants all men to be saved and to come to a knowledge of the truth" (1 Tim. 2:1–4).

It was above the ark of the covenant where God's presence dwelt. Here, the priest would intercede on behalf of Israel. Likewise, as you pray, you can intercede and petition God for the needs of others in your life.

The Tabernacle Prayer is one of many prayer models we can follow. But the key isn't to pray eloquently. You don't have to feel pressured as you pray. God won't compare your prayers to others or track the time you pray compared to the time you spend doing anything else.

Prayer comes down to your heart. It's a lifestyle. It's a posture. It's a commitment to prioritizing God and seeking His kingdom first. Because when you do, He provides for everything else (Matt. 6:33).

Scripture shows us that even Jesus would get away by Himself early in the morning or evening to pray.

> "One day Jesus was praying in a certain place" (Luke 11:1).

> "Very early in the morning, while it was still dark, Jesus got up, left the house and went off to a solitary place, where he prayed" (Mark 1:35).

There will also be times when you feel the pressures and anxieties of life crowding around you. In those moments, you have a decision to make. You can ignore it, try to cope with it, or take your worries to the Lord.

> "Humble yourselves, therefore, under God's mighty hand, that he may lift you up in due time. Cast all your anxiety on him because he cares for you. Be alert and of sober mind. Your enemy the devil prowls around like a roaring lion looking for someone to devour" (1 Pet. 5:6–8).

> "Do not be anxious about anything, but in every situation, by prayer and petition, with thanksgiving, present your requests to God. And the peace of God, which transcends all understanding, will guard your hearts and your minds in Christ Jesus" (Phil. 4:6–7).

As you develop your walk with God through your relationship with the Holy Spirit, you will also experience nudges and promptings to pray about certain things.

> "In the same way, the Spirit helps us in our weakness. We do not know what we ought to pray for, but the Spirit himself intercedes for us through wordless groans" (Rom. 8:26).

Remember, the key isn't your ability to constantly be in a state of prayer. The key is your attitude.

Here are four words that can help characterize your prayers.

Passion

"During the days of Jesus' life on earth, he offered up prayers and petitions with fervent cries and tears to the one who could save him from death, and he was heard because of his reverent submission" (Heb. 5:7).

Persistence

⁵Then Jesus said to them, 'Suppose you have a friend, and you go to him at midnight and say, 'Friend, lend me three loaves of bread; ⁶a friend of mine on a journey has come to me, and I have no food to offer him.' ⁷And suppose the one inside answers, 'Don't bother me. The door is already locked, and my children and I are in bed. I can't get up and give you anything.' ⁸I tell you, even though he will not get up and give you the bread because of friendship, yet because of your shameless audacity he will surely get up and give you as much as you need. ⁹So I say to you: Ask and it will be given to you; seek and you will find; knock and the door will be opened to you. ¹⁰For everyone who asks receives; the one who seeks finds; and to the one who knocks, the door will be opened. (Luke 11:5–10)

Partnership

"Again, truly I tell you that if two of you on earth agree about anything they ask for, it will be done for them by my Father in heaven" (Matt. 18:19).

Purpose

"And I will do whatever you ask in my name, so that the Father may be glorified in the Son. You may ask me for anything in my name, and I will do it" (Jn. 14:13–14).

Let me encourage you: pray when you get out of bed, shower, start the car, have a meeting, or go for a walk.

Everything you experience in life provides you with an opportunity to pray. This is important because, as you'll see in the next chapter, following God doesn't come without battles.

Yes, when you believe in Christ your salvation is assured. Your eternity is secure. But the enemy–the devil–will do everything he can to make sure that until you get to heaven, your life on earth feels like hell.

However, we are not without hope, victory, and a path to win these battles every time. And that's what the next chapter is all about.

GO ALL IN

- How intentional can you be about making prayer a personal and integral part of your life?
- In what areas of your life have you relied more on your strength rather than praying?
- How can prayer deepen your relationship with God and the Holy Spirit? What is something you can pray for right now?

CHAPTER 14

FINDING FREEDOM

Elephants are one of the world's strongest and most majestic creatures.

The African Bush Elephant, in particular, can weigh up to eleven tons.[18] Their trunk, comprised of over 40,000 muscles and tendons, can lift more than four hundred pounds!

Yet, a little rope can hold them down.

Elephant trainers have learned that if you tie down an elephant when they're young with a rope strong enough to keep them from getting away, they will believe that the same rope is stronger than they are.

It doesn't matter how big the elephant gets. In that elephant's mind, that simple rope is their kryptonite.

It's incredible what a lie or wrong belief can do.

You see, Jesus came that you might have life. But not just any life–abundant life (Jn. 10:10). He declared in Luke 4:18 …

> "The Spirit of the Lord is on me, because he has anointed me to proclaim good news to the poor. He has sent me to proclaim freedom for the prisoners and recovery of sight for the blind, to set the oppressed free…"

---

18   Web. https://www.nature.org/en-us/get-involved/how-to-help/animals-we-protect/african-bush-elephant/. Accessed 5 Dec, 2024.

Jesus' ministry has always been about freedom, deliverance, and abundance. He doesn't want a rope–a lie–to hold you back from His best for you. In fact, I believe there are four key things God wants for every person:

- To know Him.
- Experience freedom.
- Discover purpose.
- And make a difference.

A large portion of this book has been dedicated to knowing God. But in these last chapters, I want to devote some space to those other three, starting with freedom.

Before we discuss what that freedom looks like, let's first define what a life without freedom is characterized by.

Stolen focus

Maybe there's a dream or promise God has put in your heart to do something with your life, but you find it hard to concentrate. That might not simply be a lack of discipline. It could be a sign that the enemy has a "stronghold" in your life (2 Cor. 10:4). A stronghold is an area of your life over which the enemy still has influence.

Controlled behavior

This is the experience of continuing to do what you don't want and feeling remorseful about it. It can be an addiction or bad habit, and it can be easy to take on the identity of the sin. The Apostle Paul struggled with this. He wrote in Romans 7:15, "I do not understand what I do. For what I want to do I do not do, but what I hate I do." And yet, there is hope! Paul later wrote in that same chapter, "Thanks be to God, who delivers me through Jesus Christ our Lord!" (Rom. 7:25).

Depleted emotional energy

This can look and feel like hopelessness and depression. It's the belief or idea that no matter how hard you try, life won't get any better. Thankfully, however, you were created to live in the reality of this promise: "The path of the righteous is like the morning sun, shining ever brighter till the full light of day" (Prov. 4:18).

A lack of purpose

We'll talk about purpose specifically in the next chapter, but this characteristic is essential to recognize because the enemy isn't only concerned with where you spend eternity. If he can't stop you from getting to heaven (which he can't!), he'll try to keep you struggling on earth.

Do any of those things feel familiar to you? Have you experienced them before knowing Jesus or even to this day?

We haven't talked much about Satan in this book and that's been intentional.

He's a defeated enemy. If we only focused on him, we could quickly lose sight of Jesus, the power of His sacrifice on the cross, and our victory in Him.

That said, it's important to recognize that while the war has been won, our enemy–the devil–will still try to bring us some battles.

1 John 3:8 says, "The reason the Son of God appeared was to destroy the devil's work."

I don't believe everything that doesn't go my way in life is an attack from Satan. But I've come to believe life is a lot more spiritual than we realize. The enemy takes notice when you start taking steps toward freedom and begin living out the purpose-filled life God has called you to.

Thankfully, there's a scripture that helps us know how to respond.

"For though we live in the world, we do not wage war as the world does. The weapons we fight with are not the weapons of the world. On the contrary, they have divine power to demolish strongholds. We demolish **arguments** and every **pretension** that sets itself up against the knowledge of God, and we **take captive every thought** to make it obedient to Christ" (2 Cor. 10:3–5, emphasis added).

Before I get to those words I bolded, let me first encourage you that one of the weapons that scripture speaks to is what we just learned about in the previous chapter: Prayer! It's a God-given weapon for defeating the devil every time.

Now, an argument is a rebellious idea or attitude. A pretension is something that pretends to be the truth. Both arguments and pretensions set themselves against God's Word. And both can feel like they have power over us when we choose to believe them. But remember the rope and the elephant?

Sure, you could say the rope had some power over the elephant, at least when it was little and couldn't break it. But once the elephant was fully grown, that wasn't the case anymore. The elephant falsely believed that rope didn't just have more power but the authority to keep it in place.

Likewise, in Christ, you have final authority. You can "take captive every thought" that doesn't align with God's Word and truth.

The Apostle Paul speaks to this in Ephesians 6 when he describes what many in church call the "armor of God."

> [10]Finally, be strong in the Lord and in his mighty power. [11]Put on the full armor of God, so that you can take your stand against the devil's schemes. [12]For our struggle is not against flesh and blood, but against the rulers, against the authorities, against the powers of this dark world and against the spiritual forces of evil in the heavenly realms. [13]Therefore put on the full armor of God, so that when the day of evil comes, you may be able to stand your ground, and after you

have done everything, to stand. ¹⁴Stand firm then, with the belt of truth buckled around your waist, with the breastplate of righteousness in place, ¹⁵and with your feet fitted with the readiness that comes from the gospel of peace. ¹⁶In addition to all this, take up the shield of faith, with which you can extinguish all the flaming arrows of the evil one. ¹⁷Take the helmet of salvation and the sword of the Spirit, which is the word of God (Eph. 6:10–17).

Notice how the passage ends ...

> "And pray in the Spirit on all occasions with all kinds of prayers and requests. With this in mind, be alert and always keep on praying for all the Lord's people" (Eph. 6:18).

While prayer is communion with God, it's also a confrontation with the devil. But you can be confident you're on the winning side. So, remember the truth when you're tempted or experience thoughts that are negative, hopeless, or tempt you to sin.

> "Those who are dominated by the sinful nature think about sinful things, but those who are controlled by the Holy Spirit think about things that please the Spirit. If your sinful nature controls your mind, there is death. But if the Holy Spirit controls your mind, there is life and peace" (Rom. 8:5–6, NLT).

Life and peace sound good, right? Well, experiencing both isn't out of your reach. "When he (the devil) lies, he speaks his native language, for he is a liar and the father of lies" (Jn. 8:44).

"They were born that way."

"My dad was like that and I will be too."

"I'll never be free from this."

Each of these thoughts is a lie from the enemy. And when we expose the lie and replace it with God's truth, we defeat the liar.

Instead of believing "they were born that way," you can proclaim 2 Corinthians 5:17, "Therefore, if anyone is in Christ, the new creation has come: The old has gone, the new is here!"

You can stand on 1 Peter 1:18-19, "For you know that it was not with perishable things such as silver or gold that you were redeemed from the empty way of life handed down to you from your ancestors, but with the precious blood of Christ, a lamb without blemish or defect."

And instead of thinking addiction or bad habits will always be present in your life, you can pray the words of John 8:36, "So if the Son sets you free, you will be free indeed."

Remember, there is nothing too powerful for God. And Jesus came to give you abundant life and destroy the work of the enemy! So, in the days ahead, let me encourage you to continue going all in.

The process of healing and deliverance can take time and there are moments you'll find yourself making a mistake again. I have, but that doesn't change the truth of God's Word or your newfound identity as His child.

Go all in. Cast down every thought that doesn't align with His truth. Stand in faith on His Word. He loves you, and as we'll discover in the next chapter, He has an amazing purpose for you.

GO ALL IN

- Are there any ropes or lies that have held you back?
- How often do you struggle with a sense of helplessness or hopelessness? What truths in God's Word can help you overcome these thoughts?
- Is there a specific area where you feel controlled by past experiences or family patterns? How can you invite Jesus to bring freedom to that area?

CHAPTER 15

YOUR IDENTITY, YOUR GIFTINGS, AND YOUR PURPOSE

Things started getting blurry for me in second grade.

I couldn't see clearly—whether it was something right in front of me or far away. So, I got glasses. Bifocals, actually. And I'll never forget that first day wearing them.

On the drive home, I was completely astounded. Everything was so sharp and vivid—it felt like I was seeing the world for the first time. I could tell my mom was getting emotional watching me, seeing what a difference it made.

I share this story because it's not just our physical ability to see that makes an impact; our spiritual sight matters just as much.

So, I ask you: What is your sight like? What's your perspective? What lens are you seeing life through?

Two things influence your answers to these questions:

1. Your identity
2. Your purpose.

So many people wonder who they are and why they're on this earth. I certainly have and I bet you can admit the same. Maybe figuring those things out has been elusive for you.

Here's some good news: God's will isn't some magic spell you have to unlock, and your identity isn't a hidden gem He's keeping from you.

Right here, right now, you have the capacity and opportunity to know who you are and recognize your purpose.

The starting point is how you see life, and that's intricately related to how you see yourself.

Personally, I saw life through a performance mindset for years. Though I grew up in church and knew who God was, I didn't have a relationship with Him. I didn't understand my identity or my purpose. I thought that to please God and not go to hell, I needed to be perfect!

I had a life-changing encounter with God as a fourteen-year-old, however, and when I gave Him my life, I went all in. I discovered my calling in ministry. And as I've already shared with you, I went to Bible college after high school and have since served as a pastor.

You've gone all in. The question is: Are you still looking at your life through the lens of who you were or who God has made you to be and what He is calling you to do?

I touched on this in the previous chapter because it is critical to know what God's Word says about you when it comes to attacks and lies from the enemy.

Most people don't know how well they've been made. And not knowing that can lead to brokenness, loneliness, hurt, and confusion.

Thankfully, Psalm 139:14 gives us a powerful description of how God has created us: "I praise you because I am fearfully and wonderfully made; your works are wonderful, I know that full well."

Using that scripture as a foundation, let me encourage you to let the One who designed you define you.

Here are a few more "definitions" from scripture—

"So God created mankind in his own image, in the image of God he created them; male and female he created them" (Gen. 1:27).

"But you are a chosen people, a royal priesthood, a holy nation, God's special possession, that you may declare the praises of him who called you out of darkness into his wonderful light" (1 Pet. 2:9).

"Before I formed you in the womb I knew you, before you were born I set you apart…" (Jer. 1:5)

2 Timothy 1:9 also provides us with identity and purpose: "He has saved us and called us to a holy life—not because of anything we have done but because of his own purpose and grace. This grace was given us in Christ Jesus before the beginning of time."

Before God made you, He designed you to fit your intended purpose. Ephesians 2:10 says, "For we are God's handiwork, created in Christ Jesus to do good works, which God prepared in advance for us to do."

So, we've talked about how God designed you. Now, let's cover how He's called you, which means recognizing the ways He's gifted you.

"God has given each of you a gift from His great variety of spiritual gifts. Use them well to serve one another" (1 Pet. 4:10, NLT).

1 Corinthians 12:1,4–11 also tells us,

[1]Now about the gifts of the Spirit, brothers and sisters, I do not want you to be uninformed… [4]There are different kinds of gifts, but the same Spirit distributes them. [5]There are different kinds of service, but the same Lord. [6]There are different kinds of working, but in all of them and in everyone it is the same God at work. [7]Now to each one the manifestation of the Spirit is given for the common good. [8]To one there is given through the Spirit a message of wisdom, to another a message of knowledge by means of the same Spirit, [9]to

another faith by the same Spirit, to another gifts of healing by that one Spirit, ¹⁰to another miraculous powers, to another prophecy, to another distinguishing between spirits, to another speaking in different kinds of tongues, and to still another the interpretation of tongues. ¹¹All these are the work of one and the same Spirit, and he distributes them to each one, just as he determines.

God hasn't gifted you merely to build your platform but to build His Kingdom and help others. Keeping this in mind can also help you not to compare your gifts to someone else's.

1 Corinthians 12:12–14 says, "Just as a body, though one, has many parts, but all its many parts form one body, so it is with Christ. For we were all baptized by one Spirit so as to form one body—whether Jews or Gentiles, slave or free—and we were all given the one Spirit to drink. Even so the body is not made up of one part but of many."

Again, God hasn't only gifted you to help you thrive individually. He also wants you to benefit and build up collectively in your home, community, and church.

Maybe you've thought God's gifts are only for certain people. Maybe you don't feel qualified for God to use you. Perhaps you have some mistakes or hurts in your past that you think are too much for God to heal.

I've felt the same way. But Romans 11:29 encourages us: "God's gifts and his call are irrevocable."

The reality is we're all on a journey of following God. Right now, you're in a season of going all in and giving God a year of your life. Part of that means believing in the power of His forgiveness and salvation for you. Trust that His sacrifice on the cross was enough to save you, redeem you, and now, give you a purpose—because it is!

What's more, the same power that raised Jesus from the grave is the same power that fills you with both the gifts of the Holy Spirit and gifts to make a difference around you (see Rom. 8:11). And when you find your gifting, you will…

- Be good at it.
- Have an opportunity to use it.
- Have the capacity to develop it.
- And be energized by it.

Remember the energizer bunny? That's your passion! It makes you tick, or as my East Tennessee friends and family would say, it cranks your tractor.

But now, let's get practical. Because while your purpose involves how you can further God's kingdom in a church setting, He also wants to help you find the answers to questions like:

- Which college should I go to?
- What should my career be?
- Who should I date and eventually marry?
- Should I buy this house or this car?
- Does God even care about this stuff?

So, I want to give you ten practical tests I learned many years ago from my pastor, Jerry Lawson. These ten tests will help you determine God's purpose for you.

The Word Test

Is this consistent with Scripture? Will this violate any biblical principles? If you believe God's Word is true, then anything opposing His Word wouldn't be part of His will for your life. This test serves as a solid foundation. The Bible provides God's heart, mind, and standards, so if a choice conflicts with Scripture, it's a clear signal to stop. God's Word lights our path, guiding us through even the toughest choices (Psa. 119:105).

The Marriage Test

If you're married, your spouse's support and unity matter. Ask, is my spouse on board with this decision? When you're not aligned, it's wise to pause, pray, and wait. Otherwise, moving forward can cause strain and conflict. Ephesians 5:31 reminds us that two become one flesh in marriage, which means big decisions should be made together, with both of you at peace about it.

The Family Test

Consider the impact on your family: Will this decision bless them, or could it put them at risk? It's tempting to view certain opportunities as too good to pass up, but if they come at the cost of family stability or well-being, they might not be God's best. Jesus emphasized the importance of family relationships (Mark 10:9), and protecting your family's physical, emotional, and spiritual health is paramount.

The Peace Test

Do I have peace about going forward with this? True peace isn't merely the feeling you get when things are going great. It's what you experience when things are falling apart yet you choose to trust God despite it. Philippians 4:7 speaks of a peace that "transcends all understanding." This peace is from God and guards your heart and mind, helping you stay grounded and trust Him, even when circumstances seem difficult.

The Ministry Test

Will this move help or hinder my ability to minister for Christ? Jesus told His followers to love and serve others (Matt. 20:26-28). You'll never find God's will for your life if you are living selfishly. If a choice leads to selfish pursuits, it likely isn't in line with God's will.

The Agreement Test

Have I shared this with strong Christians in my life and are they in agreement with my feelings? Proverbs 15:22 says, "Plans fail for lack of counsel, but with many advisers they succeed." God places people in our lives to provide wisdom and a fresh perspective. Surround yourself with believers who won't just tell you what you want to hear but will speak truth into your life, even when it's hard. Sometimes others can see potential pitfalls that we're blind to.

The Financial Test

Will this decision move me to greater financial freedom so I can use God's finances as His Word says? In the same way it's God's will for you to serve, it's also His will for you to be generous. When it comes to investing, purchasing, or lending, make sure you position yourself to receive blessings and share them with others. Jesus encouraged wise management of resources (Luke 16:10–12), and when we steward well, we open ourselves to bless others.

The Faith Test

Is this causing me to step out in faith toward God? Rarely does God call us to play it safe. He calls us to take risks. Stepping out in faith can look different for everyone, but it's a reminder that God is with us as we trust Him. Moving to Wichita Falls to start a church was one of the biggest steps of faith my family and I have ever taken. But using these ten tests as a guide, we made the decision in faith, and without a doubt, God moved!

The Relationship Test

Are my relationships strong enough to withstand any stress this decision may bring? Sometimes a choice or move can be God's will but it isn't His timing. Ecclesiastes 3 reminds us that there is a time for everything. God wants us to be mindful of the strength of our relationships so that we can protect them as we make big moves. If a choice will damage a relationship, consider waiting or praying about it further.

The Christ-like Test

Does this move help me become more like Christ or take me away from Him and His church? Every decision you make should draw you closer to God, helping you to live in His purpose and plan for your life. If a choice causes you to drift from Him or His values, it's worth reconsidering.

Each of these tests can help you make decisions that align you with God's will and enhance your relationships, character, and faith. They can keep you grounded in His purpose, ensuring that every choice you make moves you toward His best for you.

Remember, God wants you to enjoy your life and make a difference in the world around you. It's what your purpose is all about. It's part of going all in, and the next chapter will only help you further.

GO ALL IN

- Are you seeing yourself and your life through the lens of who God says you are? Are old identities and doubts clouding your perspective?
- What gifts or talents has God given you? How can you use them to serve others and further His Kingdom?
- Are there areas in your life where you fear stepping out in faith? How can you trust God more to guide you in your purpose?

CHAPTER 16

3 KEYS FOR HEALTHY RELATIONSHIPS

"The grass is greener where you water it."

Have you ever heard or read that saying? It's derived from a statement by the Greek poet, Ovid, who lived in the first century B.C.

He writes, "The grain is always greener in foreign fields, and the flocks of our neighbor have richer yields."[19]

In other words, another person's life, spouse, home, car, or friends—all of it can seem better than what you might have. But the reality is that the "grass" isn't greener over there. The "grass" is greener where you put in the work to make it green!

Personally, I like to say the grass is greenest over the septic tank.

As someone who lived in the countryside of East Tennessee, plumbing wasn't the same as you might find in the city. Many homes didn't have pipes that led to a city's waste plant.

Instead, you'd find a septic tank—a literal tank buried in the ground that the home's wastewater would flow into.

The septic tank would then slowly leach out that waste into the ground around it. Or, a sewage company would need to be called to

---

19   Publius Ovid, 43 BC-17 A.D. Roman Poet, Ars Amatoria, Eigen's Political and Historical Quotations, https://quote.org/quote/the-grain-is-always-greener-in-foreign-617067. Accessed 5 December 2024.

come out and empty it. Needless to say, a septic tank is a nasty thing! And yet, that waste water is good fertilizer for the ground above it.

What's the point? Anything in your life that you want to grow and be healthy will require some work. It might be messy. You'll probably have to get dirty. But the work is worth it.

Already, you've done so much "ground"-work in this book. But as with every step on this journey, there's no substitute for going all in. And this is especially true in relationships.

Pause for a moment and consider: *What are my relationships like? What kind of friends do I have right now? What kind of friend am I?*

You are where you are based on the people you surround yourself with. Some friends were your choice, some you may have inherited based on your family. Regardless, your relationships have shaped you. And they're honestly some of the most important decisions you'll make.

Proverbs 27:19 says, "As water reflects the face, so one's life reflects the heart." I like to say that while a mirror reflects a person's face, what they're really like is shown by the kind of friends they choose. And it's what you value that most influences those decisions.

What do you value? What matters most to you in a relationship?

My wife and I have a set of values we hold highly in our relationship and family. They are—

- Love God.
- Give generously.
- Honor people.
- Lead others to Christ.

We'll reflect on these values when we make an important decision. We'll remember them at the end of most days when we gather around the dinner table with our kids and talk about our "highs and lows"—the moments during the day we're grateful for and others that were hard.

At City Hope Church, we have values that guide our relationships and help us accomplish what God has called us to do.

We love God.

God is our priority. We trust that when we seek Him first, everything else falls into place.

We love people.

God's grace is radical. We show the same grace to others that we have received from Him.

We give generously.

We hold nothing back. We live with eternity in mind by choosing to give above and beyond.

We pursue excellence.

We go the extra mile. We hold ourselves to a higher standard because of Who we serve.

We choose joy.

We have fun. We find reasons to celebrate because church should be enjoyed, not endured.

Whether you realize it or not, you have a set of values that govern your life—for good or bad.

If your life is filled with drama, you value drama. If your life is filled with peace, you value peace. A value is something you choose every day. Because of this, we must ensure we're valuing the right things, including *healthy* relationships.

Here are some choices that will help you make healthy relationships both a priority and a reality in your life.

CHOICE #1
Disconnect from Harmful Relationships

I read a story one time about a man who dialed the wrong number and got the following recording: "I am not available right now, but I thank you for caring enough to call. I am making some changes in my life. Please leave a message after the beep. If I do not return your call, you are one of the changes."[20]

It's a humorous story but it illustrates a necessary decision.

- To put an end to those flirtatious encounters at work.
- To stop that relationship which is causing you to compromise.
- To step away from social media and the gossip and slander it often involves.

Any relationship that pulls you away from God—and pulls you away from your spouse, if you're married—is a relationship that needs to end.

The book of Proverbs offers much counsel and many principles for nurturing relationships that help, encourage, and empower us to do this. Proverbs 5, 6, and 7 especially. Let me quickly summarize each one.

Proverbs 5

This chapter warns against the dangers of adultery and the consequences of giving in to temptation.

Verses 1 and 2 notably begin, "My son, pay attention to my wisdom, turn your ear to my words of insight, that you may maintain discretion and your lips may preserve knowledge."

Proverbs 5 is a letter from a father to their son but the wisdom shared is universal. The chapter describes the allure of an immoral

---

20   Web. https://ministry127.com/resources/illustrations/friendship. Accessed 5 Dec, 2024.

person as deceptively sweet but ultimately leading to bitterness, pain, and destruction.

The father also encourages his son to find satisfaction in his own marriage, to rejoice in the wife of his youth (Prov. 5:18).

Integrity in a relationship—especially in marriage—matters to God. And that integrity can lead to blessing and joy. Disregarding it can bring self-inflicted destruction.

I'll never forget when my pastor, Jerry Lawson, had our staff copy Proverbs 5 word for word after someone close to us had a moral failure. That moment has always stuck with me.

Proverbs 6

Here, the author provides practical advice about various aspects of life, but many impact relational health. For example:

- In verses 1 through 5 we read a warning against co-signing debts for others and to free oneself financially.
- Verses 6 through 11 highlight the values of diligence and hard work over laziness.
- We also find a list in verses 16 through 19 of seven things the Lord detests:
    1. haughty eyes,
    2. a lying tongue,
    3. hands that kill the innocent,
    4. a heart that plots evil,
    5. feet that race to do wrong,
    6. a false witness who pours out lies,
    7. a person who sows discord in a family (NLT).

Not coincidentally, each of these things can negatively impact a relationship!

Proverbs 7

This chapter vividly illustrates the danger of falling into temptation and the need to guard one's heart. "Keep my commands and you will live" (Prov. 7:2). That's how vital this wisdom is!

Verses 6 through 23 then tell the story of a young man lured by a seductive woman. This young man thinks he's in control. He believes this one-night-stand of a relationship won't harm their future. When, in reality, "it will cost him his life" (Prov. 7:23).

I encourage you, in fact, I beg you, don't delay severing any relationships that don't build you up in your marriage and help you in your relationship with God. Even now, take a moment and read Proverbs 5, 6, and 7, and let God speak to you further about them.

Proverbs 13:20 says, "Walk with the wise and become wise, for a companion of fools suffers harm." And 1 Corinthians 15:33 further implores us, "Do not be misled: Bad company corrupts good character."

CHOICE #2
Dedicate Time for Meaningful Relationships

Rarely is something easy and worthwhile. Relationships aren't. And they often require the one thing that no one has been able to buy or acquire more of: *time*.

I don't share that with you to be discouraging. I want to help you realize that meaningful relationships require intention and sacrifice. Perhaps this is why Hebrews 10:25 notably states, "And let us not neglect our meeting together, as some people do, but encourage one another, especially now that the day of his return is drawing near" (NLT).

This scripture denotes a human tendency to take the easy option and forego what it takes for a relationship to thrive. But think of it like attending church. While it isn't always easy or convenient, it's part of doing life with God. It's part of going all in.

One of the best places I know to develop relationships is in church, especially in small groups.

The next chapter is dedicated to that very thing. Still, right now, I hope you will join me in both the realization and commitment that to develop meaningful relationships, you need to prioritize them and dedicate time to them.

CHOICE #3
Intentionally Develop Important Relationships

This is where the rubber meets the road. Or, more aptly, how to make the grass in your life and relationships *green*. "Therefore be alert and of sober mind so that you may pray. Above all, love each other deeply, because love covers over a multitude of sins" (1 Pet. 4:7-8).

Loving others deeply, the kind of love that "covers over a multitude of sins," isn't an easy or passive love. It's a love that's voluntary, sacrificial, and unconditional. It's a love that isn't naive about the work relationships involve but accepts that work is part of the process.

Think of it like a fireplace. It isn't a fireplace's fault if no fire exists. You need wood, kindling, and a lighter or match to get the fire going. It takes a little work. So, let me give you two ways you can go to work in your relationships right now.

1. Be an encourager

To be an encourager is to call out the best in others. And it's hard to do that without words. So tell the people in your life, "You're a great dad." "You're an amazing mom." "I'm so proud of you." "Your smile lights up a room."

The word encourage is often translated as "comfort." I love that because I know that whenever I've been on the receiving end of someone encouraging me, that's exactly how I feel—comforted.

2 Corinthians 13:11 says, "Finally, brothers and sisters, rejoice! Strive for full restoration, encourage one another, be of one mind, live in peace. And the God of love and peace will be with you."

1 Thessalonians 5:11 says, "Therefore encourage one another and build each other up, just as in fact you are doing."

Being an encourager is a choice we have to make. Today, decide that you will build others up and not tear them down. Be an encourager!

2. Choose Unity

Now, unity isn't to be confused with uniformity. Unity isn't about getting others to act like you or even agree with you on everything. It's about moving and growing in the same direction.

Romans 12:16 teaches us, "Live in harmony with one another. Do not be proud, but be willing to associate with people of low position. Do not be conceited."

When I reflect on the relationships in my life that have taken work, my marriage comes to mind more than anything else.

I have a fantastic wife. I like to say that living with Annaliese is like living with an angel. But that doesn't mean our marriage is easy.

Back in 2020, we had a goal to go on a date once per week. We needed to do it because we were struggling amidst the COVID-19 pandemic and serving in ministry. We reflected on two things:

1. The devil hates our marriage and wants to destroy it.

2. The grass is greener over the septic tank.

Our relationship wasn't going to thrive by itself. We had to make choices that would propel us in the direction we wanted to go.

I've heard my friend, Pastor Chris Hodges, say it this way: Choices lead, feelings follow. So, make choices that will nurture your most important relationships.

Remember those family values I shared with you earlier? Those have been a great way for my wife and I to take inventory of ourselves and our relationship. We'll ask ourselves and discuss together—

- How is my relationship with God?
- Am I being generous with my time, talent, and treasure?
- Am I honoring the people around me in my home, workplace, church, and community?
- Am I leading others to Christ?

Whether you're married or single, asking yourself questions like those is an effective way to grow in your relational health and give the Holy Spirit room to speak to you and help you!

GO ALL IN

- What relationships in your life need more attention? Reflect on where you may have been neglecting important relationships. What specific actions can you take to nurture them?
- Are there any harmful relationships you need to remove to cultivate a healthier environment for growth? Consider whether people or other influences are pulling you away from your values or goals. What steps can you take to create better boundaries?
- What values are guiding your relationships? Do they align with the life you want to live?
- What "choices" can you make today to help your relationships thrive, regardless of your current feelings? Identify small, actionable steps you can commit to, even if they require discipline and sacrifice.

CHAPTER 17

GET IN A SMALL GROUP

Yola grew up going to church on Sundays, but her family didn't think or talk much about God for the rest of the week. Yola believed God was legalistic and that when she got to Heaven, He would be mad at her for the bad things she did. She compared Him to her earthly father, who would only condemn her when she messed up.

"When I disappointed my dad, he would sit me down at the dining room table and list out all the ways I disappointed him. I remember once, when I was twelve, he had me at the table for five hours listing my disappointments."

Yola's father would also get emotionally and physically abusive, and when she got pregnant when she was sixteen, he kicked her out of the house. She had to live in a home for unwed mothers.

Months later, Yola had her son and because her dad loved *him*, he let them return to the house under one condition: She had to keep her baby boy quiet whenever visitors came over.

"No one could know about my son. It would ruin the image of our 'perfect' family. I got married just to leave the house and had my daughter. My family would go to church on and off but never experienced much joy… then City Hope Church came to town! My sister and I began attending on launch day. I have never experienced so much joy being exuded from a church. I know that when I left the service on launch day, I felt different. I was happy. Pastor Ben talked about giving God a year and I like a challenge! I went through Growth Track, began serving, and joined a Freedom small group. Freedom changed my life. I didn't realize all the pain I was carrying… I began to serve on the greeting team and in our community. I was reading my Bible and having real conversations about The Word. I love my life and have a relationship with God. I know He is not the 'mean' God I thought he was but a loving Father who hurts when I hurt and rejoices in my accomplishments! I gave God a Year and He has given me my life!"

What a heartbreaking yet beautiful story of what God can do when a person—regardless of their past or present circumstances—decides to give God a year, go all in, and see what He can do.

I love how Yola didn't hold anything back. She attended church faithfully. She went through "Growth Track," a three-week class at City Hope that helps people become members and practically learn how to live life as followers of Jesus. Yola served, which is something we'll focus more on in a later chapter. She prioritized reading the Bible. Yola joined a small group and had "real conversations about the Word."

Not coincidentally, the lives of New Testament believers looked similar to Yola's. They would attend "church" at the synagogue, then go from house to house, meeting, encouraging, and worshiping God together.

Acts 2:44 says, "All the believers met together constantly and shared everything with each other" (Holy Bible, Living Bible Translation).

In the comfort of their home, surrounded by a "small group" of like-minded friends, they shared life—talking about Scripture, what God was doing in their lives, their struggles, hopes, dreams, questions, and the discoveries they were making along the way.

These early Christians didn't merely see each other once a week on Sundays. They did life *together*.

I've been referring to the church I pastor as City Hope throughout this book but our website and legal name is City Hope Family. We intentionally chose to use the word family because that's what we're trying to build—*family!*

"Now you are no longer strangers to God and foreigners to heaven, but you are members of God's very own family, citizens of God's country, and you belong in God's household with every other Christian" (Eph. 2:19, TLB).

Remember, as we learned in an earlier chapter, when you became a Christian, you became part of a new family, a spiritual one called the church. And, like any family, things can get messy.

No family is perfect, and no church is faultless. However, I want to encourage you to find a church home and commit to loving the people around you and fight *for* them, not *with* them.

I don't know any better way to do this than in a small group.

As I've mentioned, a small group is nothing more than meeting with a "small group" of believers in a home, coffee shop, or other setting. And there are a few things small groups help with in particular.

1. Take Off The Mask

2 Corinthians 3:18 says, "So all of us who have had that veil removed can see and reflect the glory of the Lord. And the Lord—who is the Spirit—makes us more and more like him as we are changed into his glorious image" (NLT).

Following Jesus means becoming like Him, but we live in a culture of filters and highlight reels. Due to expectations placed on us by others and the world, we can find ourselves trading who we are for a mask of what other people might want us to be (or even a part of ourselves we want to hide).

Some wear a mask of shame. Others wear a mask that will get them the approval of others. I wore a mask of perfection and performance for years. I believed the lie that I would never have enough or be good enough.

I went to church multiple days of the week. I played the part of a "good Christian." I said the right things, acted the right way, and wore the right clothes. All the while, my heart was hiding. I wasn't opening up. No one knew my deepest dreams or struggles.

That's what small groups are for. They provide an intimate, dedicated space to be open, vulnerable, and encouraged. Of course, Sundays at church are important. But in a small group you can take off any mask you're wearing and be known.

2. Grow Spiritually

Yola's story demonstrates this point so powerfully. She specifically joined a small group that went through a twelve-week study about freedom. She further shared…

> "I had shame from being a teenage mother. I was promiscuous into adulthood, binge drinking alcohol, quick to anger, and had no real joy. I slowly began to change (for the better)… I laid all my pain, all my disappointments, and all my guilt at God's feet, and I am a new person. I have true joy in my heart."

In other words, Yola took off her mask. She didn't hide. She allowed the people around her to know the real her, love her where she was, and help her move forward in her faith.

In Jeremiah 29:13 God promises, "If you look for me wholeheartedly, you will find me" (NLT). The opposite is also true. If you don't look for God wholeheartedly or take off the mask, you won't find Him, others won't know you, and you won't have the opportunity to grow.

The choice is yours, just as it was for Yola.

Now, I do recognize that this choice is a vulnerable one. There's a risk of being hurt. But while the risk may be real, think of the reward!

God has so many wonderful things He wants to do in your life. Again, Yola's story shows this so beautifully. So let me encourage you: Take the risk. Take off the mask. It's how you will grow into the person God made you to be.

3. Move Forward In Your Purpose

Just two chapters ago, we dove into the topic of your purpose and gifting, but let me reiterate: To do what God is calling you to do, you need the help and encouragement of other people. And small groups provide such an effective space for this.

Yola shared how she had conversations about the Word, and I'm confident those conversations helped her better understand who God is and how He was calling her forward.

I can't tell you how many times someone has said to me, "Well, I tried Christianity, and it didn't work for me." My immediate thought is usually, *Of course, it didn't work. You didn't go All IN!*

I wish I could have a face-to-face conversation with you right now. I'd love to know how your life has already transformed from the moment you picked up this book. But even though I can't, I *can* encourage you to attend church faithfully, read the Word, pray, embrace the Holy Spirit, nurture healthy relationships, and join a small group.

Trust me: you won't regret going all in!

There's no substitute for it. God isn't satisfied with half-hearted commitment or a life devoted to Him some or even most of the time. He wants it all. He needs it all because only then can He take the broken pieces of our lives and make something entirely new and wonderful.

Interestingly, a man in scripture thought he *was* living all in.

He considered himself an expert when it came to living for God, so when Jesus came along and started preaching, teaching, and performing miracles, this "expert" was both curious and pessimistic. He tested Jesus with some questions. He probably thought Jesus would feel stumped or cornered by a man who so clearly and confidently had it all together.

But not Jesus. And what He shared in response to those questions is the next step on our journey to giving God a year.

GO ALL IN

- What "masks" do you wear that prevent others from knowing the real you? Think about any ways you may be hiding behind a facade of acceptance, approval, or self-protection. What would it look like to open up in a safe space?
- Consider who challenges and supports you in your faith journey. How can you invest more in these connections?
- What small group or community can you join that would help you take off the mask, grow in your faith, and discover your purpose?

CHAPTER 18

HOW TO LOVE

When a self-proclaimed expert asked Jesus about eternal life, he thought he knew the answer. He was looking for affirmation, not transformation.

But Jesus doesn't just respond to questions—He reveals the deeper issues of the heart. And at that moment, He turned the tables on the conversation, offering a simple and revolutionary perspective.

The story that follows is one of the most famous parables in Scripture: the story of the Good Samaritan. But don't miss the weight of what led to it. It wasn't just a question about "who is my neighbor?" but about what it really means to love God with everything we are.

WHAT'S THE QUESTION REALLY ABOUT?

Luke 10:25–35 introduces us to a conversation between Jesus and an expert in the law, one that ultimately challenges us to reexamine what it means to truly love. Here's how the exchange unfolds—

> [25]On one occasion an expert in the law stood up to test Jesus. 'Teacher,' he asked, 'what must I do to inherit eternal life?' [26]'What is written in the Law?' he replied. 'How do you read it?' [27]He answered, 'Love the Lord your God with all your heart and with all your soul and with all your strength and with all your mind'; and, 'Love your neighbor as yourself.'"

[28]'You have answered correctly,' Jesus replied. 'Do this and you will live.' [29]But he wanted to justify himself (This expert not only wanted to feel good about himself, he wanted everyone hearing this conversation to know just how good of a person he was!), so he asked Jesus, 'And who is my neighbor?'

[30]'In reply Jesus said, 'A man was going down from Jerusalem to Jericho, when he was attacked by robbers. They stripped him of his clothes, beat him and went away, leaving him half dead. [31]A priest happened to be going down the same road, and when he saw the man, he passed by on the other side. [32]So too, a Levite, when he came to the place and saw him, passed by on the other side.

[33]But a Samaritan, as he traveled, came where the man was; and when he saw him, he took pity on him. [34]He went to him and bandaged his wounds, pouring on oil and wine. Then he put the man on his own donkey, brought him to an inn and took care of him. [35]The next day he took out two denarii and gave them to the innkeeper. 'Look after him,' he said, 'and when I return, I will reimburse you for any extra expense you may have.'

We've been discovering what it looks like to develop healthy relationships and experience the community small groups bring. In other words, we've been discussing how to love people, especially those close to us—spouses, friends, and family.

But what about the people you disagree with, don't like, or perhaps don't like you? What does it look like to give God a year in that context?

IDENTIFYING YOURSELF IN THE STORY

Jesus' story—"The Parable of the Good Samaritan"—answers those questions. It's a story filled with meaning and practical application. And I think it's essential to first identify ourselves in it.

The first character is the man left for dead on the road

Now, while you may have never found yourself beaten and bloodied next to a highway, I'm sure there has been a moment when you felt alone, hurt, and unsure how to carry on.

- Perhaps you received some bad news from the doctor.
- Your marriage was on the brink of collapse.
- A child was estranged.
- A friend abandoned or betrayed you.
- Financially, you were in over your head.

I've faced those kinds of challenges. I've needed help. We all do sometimes.

The Priest or Levite

These are two guys who could have done something. They *should* have done something.

They had the means to help but didn't want to be bothered or inconvenienced. It wasn't an issue of time but sacrifice. It wasn't about resources but a willingness to offer help.

The Samaritan

If anybody had an excuse not to help, it was the Samaritan. After all, the Samaritans were at odds with Israel. There was extreme prejudice, distrust, and hate on both sides. And yet, the Samaritan didn't ignore this seeming enemy.

He put differences aside, ignored the excuses, and responded with compassion.

The Innkeeper

The Samaritan commissioned the Innkeeper to carry on the work of healing.

We can step into this role when someone other than us may have been the first to offer help in a crisis but later join after recognizing the need and wanting to be a part of the solution. And lastly—

The Donkey

Including the donkey's role may seem humorous, but I'm serious! The donkey played a role in this story, too. It was on the donkey the beaten and bruised man was carried to the inn. Sometimes, that can be you and me. We can find ourselves in a position where we carry a load for someone else.

After Jesus told the story, He didn't point out all five characters like I did. He highlighted three. He asked the expert, "'Which of these three do you think was a neighbor to the man who fell into the hands of robbers?' The expert in the law replied, 'The one who had mercy on him.' Jesus told him, 'Go and do likewise'" (Luke 10:36–37).

Notice that Jesus didn't shame the priest or Levite, both of whom could have helped. He didn't say the Samaritan should've had a wagon instead of a donkey to carry the man.

Jesus' words are always life-giving. He points toward the kingdom. And He's letting this expert know how to give God a year. He's showing him, and us, what it looks like on a practical level to live a life marked by love.

LOVE IN ACTION

There are four things we can learn about love from the Good Samaritan.

Love cares

The Samaritan didn't just look at the man—he saw him. Compassion begins when we truly see people, not just their circumstances.

Luke 10:33 says, "Then a despised Samaritan came along. And when he **saw** the man, he felt **compassion** for him (emphasis added)."

Remember, Samaritans and Jews were at odds. A "normal" Samaritan wouldn't have felt compassion towards a Jew who was hurt. But he saw him. He didn't turn away from the plight of this beaten and bloodied man. He was moved to action. He didn't see a Jew. He saw a man in trouble. And he cared.

Love gets close

Think about that for a moment. The Bible says the priest and Levite turned and walked away upon seeing the man. But the Samaritan saw the man and knelt beside him. He got close.

Something powerful happens when we don't just acknowledge a person is in trouble but get close to understand the whole picture.

Proximity matters. It's easy to avoid helping when we keep our distance. But when we get close, we can hear, see, and understand the needs of others.

Closeness creates the opportunity for compassion. And compassion is more than just knowing the need. Compassion recognizes the need and says, "I have to do something about this."

Love is committed to the process

> "He went to him and bandaged his wounds, pouring on oil and wine. Then he put the man on his own donkey, brought him to an inn and took care of him" (Luke 10:34).

Healing takes time. The Samaritan didn't stop at first aid—he saw the process through, ensuring the man was in a safe space to recover.

Similarly, there's a process God wants to bring about in you and me to heal and restore us to the people He made us to be. That's why we give Him a year. That's why we go all in. It's how a lifestyle of walking with Jesus is formed that leads to eternal life.

Philippians 1:6 puts it this way, "Being confident of this, that he who began a good work in you will carry it on to completion until the day of Christ Jesus."

Love doesn't give up hope

The Samaritan told the Innkeeper to continue looking after the man, even promising him that he'd return and reimburse any further expenses (Luke 10:35).

I believe the Samaritan said this because he expected the man to recover. Despite his beaten and bloody condition, he was full of hope for the man's future.

What is hope? It's a desire and expectation that good things will happen. And because of Jesus, we can always be full of hope. Romans

8:28 assures us, "And we know that in all things God works for the good of those who love him, who have been called according to his purpose."

So, for a moment, reflect on your life. Have you lived with the kind of love the Good Samaritan demonstrated to those around you?

Loving others is undoubtedly a calling on our lives from God. The phrase "love one another" appears twelve times in the New Testament. And it isn't a suggestion. It's a command. Jesus said in John 13:34–35,

> "A new command I give you: Love one another. As I have loved you, so you must love one another. By this everyone will know that you are my disciples, if you love one another."

Here are a few more examples:

> "Owe nothing to anyone—except for your obligation to love one another. If you love your neighbor, you will fulfill the requirements of God's law" (Rom. 13:8, NLT).

> "Be completely humble and gentle; be patient, bearing with one another in love"(Eph. 4:2).

> "And may the Lord make your love for one another and for all people grow and overflow…" (1 Thess. 3:12, NLT).

Whether you find someone hurt on the side of the road or comfort a neighbor crying on their front porch, be willing to help and love people where they are.

Few things matter as much as love, but many things will fall into place *as* you love. And while we'll discover what it looks like to serve others in the next chapter, any form of service honestly won't mean a thing if we first don't understand *how* to love.

> "[4]Love is patient, love is kind. It does not envy, it does not boast, it is not proud. [5]It does not dishonor others, it is not self-seeking, it is not easily angered, it keeps no record of wrongs. [6]Love does not delight in evil but rejoices with the truth. [7]It always protects, always trusts, always hopes, always perseveres. [8]Love never fails …

¹³And now these three remain: faith, hope and love. But the greatest of these is love" (1 Cor. 13:4–8, 13).

Let me encourage you to once again receive God's amazing love for you. And as you continue giving Him a year, let it inspire your love for others.

GO ALL IN

- Which character in the story of the Good Samaritan do you most relate to and why?
- How do you respond when faced with opportunities to help someone in need, especially when it's inconvenient? What steps can you take to ensure compassion guides your actions?
- How can you get "closer" to people in need around you instead of staying at a safe distance?
- Are you committed to the "process" of loving others, even when it requires ongoing effort? Do you hold onto hope for others, believing God can work all things for their good?

CHAPTER 19

THE DREAM TEAM

Imagine waking up with $86,400 automatically deposited into your bank account each day. Sounds good, right?

A few conditions:

- You can't roll it over into the next day.
- You can't save it.
- You can't transfer it.
- You have to spend it every day or it's gone forever.

Still interested? Well, it may not be money, but 86,400 *seconds* is the exact amount of time you have daily. And just like that illustration, you can't save, transfer, or roll it over. Every day, those seconds have no choice but to come and go. But you *do* have a choice as to how you spend them.

In this second to last chapter, I want to make the case for you to devote many of those precious seconds to serving others.

The Parable of the Good Samaritan is a beautiful picture of this because it was out of the Samaritan's love for others that he was compelled by compassion to *serve* others.

The same needs to be true for you and me.

Paul, a friend and member of City Hope Church, shared a story with me as I wrote this book about how serving sparked a passion and purpose he had never experienced before.

"City Hope was in 21 days of Prayer and Fasting. I went on a 21-day juice fast. Within days of completing that, my wife and I found ourselves in a 1st Saturday Serve day. We served again the following month and visited a service after that. From that point on, City Hope has been our church home. We'd planned to move away after the kids finished high school, but we found a new family at City Hope that is constantly growing. We can't imagine leaving. City Hope has been our home ever since, and we are going all in from now on."

That Serve Day Paul referred to is something City Hope has been doing for years now.

As a church family, we dedicate the first Saturday of every month to loving people in our local community by serving them. This can include sharing meals, helping with a building project, or picking trash up beside streets.

Then, every week at our church services, we have our Dream Team. Through the City Hope Dream Team, we connect every person to an opportunity to grow in their calling.

I could share some examples of what the Dream Team looks like, but it's about more than a task, obligation, or job. It's about serving one another, no matter what that "serving" looks like.

So often we can look at family, friendships, and situations, asking, *What's in this for me?* But a heart of service puts the needs of others before your own.

Ultimately, when you serve others, you're serving Jesus.

> "The King will reply, 'Truly I tell you, whatever you did for one of the least of these brothers and sisters of mine, you did for me'" (Matt. 25:40).

Not coincidentally, studies have been done on the impact serving others has on a person's well-being. The findings are remarkable. Here's what Berkely College discovered—

> Giving social support—time, effort, or goods—is associated with better overall health in older adults, and

volunteering is associated with delayed mortality. Generosity appears to have especially strong associations with psychological health and well-being. For example, a meta-analysis of 37 studies of older adults found that those who volunteered reported greater quality of life; another study found that frequent helpers reported feeling greater vitality and self-esteem (but only if they chose to help of their own accord). Other studies have shown a link between generosity and happiness. Some studies have found that people are happier when spending money on others than on themselves, and this happiness motivates them to be generous in the future. And even small acts of kindness, like picking up something someone else has dropped, make people feel happy. Generosity is also associated with benefits in the workplace, such as reducing the likelihood of job burnout, and in relationships, where it is associated with more contentment and longer-lasting romantic relationships.[21]

Clearly, serving others has its rewards. And living like Jesus means we're committed to loving *and* serving others.

It's not that God isn't able to do whatever He wants to do on the earth. After all, he's God! The reality, however, is that He chose to accomplish His purpose and plan through imperfect people like you and me. And if God wants to work through us, I want to experience that, don't you?

After all, if not us, then who? If not now, when? If not here, where?

Even the smallest acts of serving make a difference. Matthew 10:42 says, "And if anyone gives even a cup of cold water to one of these little ones because he is my disciple, I tell you the truth, he will certainly not lose his reward."

---

21 Web. https://ggsc.berkeley.edu/images/uploads/GGSC-JTF_White_Paper-Generosity-FINAL.pdf. Accessed 6 Dec, 2024.

It ultimately comes down to your time, talent, and treasure. I've been referring to those three words throughout this book, but now we're going to understand their meaning in the context of serving.

1. Time

We all have the same amount of time. Remember, 86,400 seconds every day. So, ask yourself: *Am I making the most of my time? Am I using some of my time to serve others?*

We don't have to endure constant pressure or stress to get something done every waking moment. "There is a time for everything, and a season for every activity under the heavens" (Eccl. 3:1).

When it's time to rest or have fun with your family, dedicate your time to do so. But also prioritize spending time with God and *serving* others.

2. Talent

Your "Talent" is defined by your gifting and passion. It's what drives you, excites you, and motivates you to action. And scripture is clear: God doesn't want your talent to remain hidden.

In Matthew 25:14-30, Jesus told a parable about talents. In the story, talent was a term for money, but the principle regarding your gifting and passion is the same.

You see, a master had three servants. And when it was time for him to leave on a trip, he gave one servant one talent, one two talents, and another five talents.

Now, the person with one talent was afraid to lose it and chose to do nothing with it. He hid it, burying it in the ground.

The second servant doubled his five talents. And the third servant did the same.

When the master returned, he was pleased with the two servants who multiplied what he had given them. But to the servant who did nothing and hid their talent out of fear, the master was displeased.

What's the lesson? When it comes to the *talent* God has given you, steward it well. Don't hide in fear. Serve others and use your talent for His glory!

3. Treasure

Treasure isn't about what you accumulate here on earth. It's about what you store up in heaven.

Matthew 6:19-20 says, "Do not store up for yourselves treasures on earth, where moths and vermin destroy, and where thieves break in and steal. But store up for yourselves treasures in heaven, where moths and vermin do not destroy, and where thieves do not break in and steal."

There's no mistaking that generosity is our calling, not just by giving through our tithe but also by our acts of kindness toward others.

Brenda's story reflects this. She visited City Hope Church one weekend, and when someone on our Dream Team prayed for her, she experienced grace, kindness, and love. And it changed her life.

"A woman asked me if I needed prayer, Sandra Lea. I explained what I was going through, and she prayed for me... I gave God a year, and the blessings have just poured out. I would have never thought I would be serving on the Baptism Dream team, going out on Serve Day, or part of a small group. I have changed so much since attending City Hope. I have met so many people and done so much with them that I am still in awe. Honestly, I can't write everything that God has done in my life in one year, but I do know Mrs. Sandra Lea was put in my path for a reason." – Brenda

I love that story and seeing what God is doing in Brenda's life and how He worked through Mrs. Sandra Lea. That's the power of serving and being a part of the Dream Team.

The fact is, you don't have to attend City Hope to serve. You can join the "Dream Team" right where you are and be an example of God's love, grace, and hope in your neighborhood and community today!

So, reflect on your time, talent, and treasure. How are your seconds being spent? What (or who) are you investing in? Are you faithful in the little things—the moments and situations that perhaps no one else sees?

In Luke 16:10, Jesus said, "Whoever can be trusted with very little can also be trusted with much, and whoever is dishonest with very little will also be dishonest with much."

There will be more days you *don't* feel like serving others than days you *do* feel like it. But we don't live by feelings or pressure. We live by *principle*.

Even if you don't have all the money in the world to renovate your local library or build a shelter for people experiencing homelessness, utilize what you have right now. Choose to serve no matter how little or big it seems.

Wake up early on your day off to meet the needs of someone struggling to meet their own needs. Mow a lawn. Buy someone a coffee. Volunteer in your community and local church.

Give of your time, talent, and treasure. When you have a willing heart, there's no limit to what God will do. And as we'll discover in the final chapter of our journey together, you can also experience immense *joy* in the process.

GO ALL IN

- Reflect on how you spend your time each day—the unique gifts and abilities God has given you, and the resources you steward. Are you using them to make a difference?
- What is holding you back from fully embracing a lifestyle of serving others? Consider any fears, excuses, or distractions that prevent you from stepping out to serve.
- Who in your life or community could benefit from an act of kindness today?

CHAPTER 20

CHOOSE JOY

Life is filled with choices.

You chose to pick up this book and read it. You chose to give God a year. You chose to make Jesus the Lord of your life. That last choice is probably the most powerful because Jesus chose first, out of His love for you, to sacrifice Himself for your salvation, healing, and redemption.

Choices. We all have them. History is defined by them. And before we conclude our journey together of giving God a year, there's one more choice I want to encourage you to make that's also an integral value of City Hope Church—

Choose joy

You may remember me mentioning that value back in Chapter 16. It may seem out of place, like something helpful, but not as important as other things.

From the moment you decided to give God a year, each step has prepared you for this choice—to embrace the joy found in surrender and trust. Choosing joy is not just a single act; it's a daily decision that is rooted in everything you've learned.

Friend, I can't emphasize enough just how consequential choosing joy is. Church, let alone *life*, isn't something to be endured. It's to be enjoyed!

Psalm 118:24 says, "This is the day the Lord has made. We will rejoice and be glad in it" (NLT). And in Psalm 16:11 we read, "You make known to me the path of life; you will fill me with joy in your presence, with eternal pleasures at your right hand."

In this final chapter, I want to give you a practical key to help you choose *and experience* joy no matter what life brings your way. Ready?

Let the balloon go.

My wife, Annaliese, and I have four sons. Each of their personalities are different. Each is uniquely gifted. Some have experienced the same struggles. Others have overcome new ones. But there are four words my sons hear from their mom whenever life gets stressful or uncertain.

Let the balloon go.

Imagine you're holding a balloon tied to a string in your hand. The only thing keeping that balloon from flying into the sky is your ability to hold onto it.

Life's stresses and struggles aren't too different from that picture. Often, the only thing keeping us stuck in a messy mindset or state of stress is our stubbornness, or at times unwillingness, to let go of control and trust God.

He wants to help but we try to figure it out. He has the provision and peace we need, yet we look for solutions ourselves. We hold onto the string. Meanwhile, God is inviting us—

Let the balloon go.

In Matthew 11:28-29 Jesus said, "Come to me, all you who are weary and burdened, and I will give you rest. Take my yoke upon you and learn from me, for I am gentle and humble in heart, and you will find rest for your souls."

Life with God isn't meant to be toilsome or wearying. Yes, there will be seasons when life gets busy and you're tired. But ultimately, joy is yours to receive in Christ.

My wife preached a message one time about this very thing, and one of my favorite quotes she shared was this:

> *"Joy isn't about getting our way;*
> *it's about yielding to God's way."*

The key is to let the balloon go. So, I want to focus for a moment on another word that describes letting go and that's *release*.

Release means "to allow or enable to escape from confinement, to set free, to allow something to move, act, or flow freely." When we release a situation or struggle to God, we make room for Him to move freely in whatever it is.

- It could be a situation involving your kids.
- A problem at work.
- A financial debt.
- An argument with a friend.

When you release something, you choose the path of joy by letting the balloon go and *releasing* your concern to God. You might not feel joy in the moment but releasing sets you on the path *towards* it.

I think about when Annaliese's dad passed away in 2006.

It was a very traumatic time for our family. He had a massive heart attack and Annaliese's mom found him on the floor of their bedroom. It was horrible and heartbreaking. But I can attest that Annaliese's mom consciously released the situation to God.

Yes, there was sadness. The grief was real. But so also was the peace of God.

Let me encourage you: If you're finding yourself at the end of our journey together desiring more peace and joy, or perhaps hoping the peace and joy you have now will last—

Let the balloon go.

What are you holding onto? What are you not allowing God to do in your life? What are you not releasing?

Are you holding on to unforgiveness? Are you trying to maintain hanging on to performance and perfectionism? Are you worried about your health or finances?

In 1 Samuel 25, we find David struggling with this very thing.

You see, a wealthy man named Nabal had thousands of goats and sheep. David also had a lot of livestock and they shared grazing fields. David had ensured his men were always kind to Nabal and never took any of his sheep or goats for their own.

It came time to shear the wool off the sheep and David's men were in need of food and water, and Nabal was the nearest source of help. So, David sent a message asking for help.

Nabal answered David's servants, "Who is this David? Who is this son of Jesse? Many servants are breaking away from their masters these days. Why should I take my bread and water, and the meat I have slaughtered for my shearers, and give it to men coming from who knows where?" (1 Sam. 25:10-11).

When word of Nabal's response got back to David, he was insulted and angry. Immediately, he prepared four hundred men for battle to kill Nabal and every male in his household. Talk about revenge!

Nabal's wife, Abigail, also heard about Nabal's response. Unlike her husband, she was kind and discerning. She gathered gifts, food, animals, and water, then met David before he could attack.

Abigail asked David for forgiveness on behalf of her husband. She said, "When the Lord has fulfilled for my lord every good thing he promised concerning him and has appointed him ruler over Israel, my lord will not have on his conscience the staggering burden of needless bloodshed or of having avenged himself. And when the Lord your God has brought my lord success, remember your servant" (1 Sam. 25:30-31).

David still could have been mad at Nabal. After all, he hadn't apologized. His wife had! But David said in return, "Praise be to the Lord, the God of Israel, who has sent you today to meet me. May you be blessed for your good judgment and for keeping me from bloodshed this day and from avenging myself with my own hands. Otherwise, as surely as the Lord, the God of Israel, lives, who has kept me from harming you, if you had not come quickly to meet me, not one male belonging to Nabal would have been left alive by daybreak" (1 Sam. 25:32–34).

Of course, it has never been God's desire for us to settle disputes with one another by means of attack or revenge.

David's example is a dramatic one, but no less powerful. And about ten days after all this happened, Nabal died on his own, with no guilt or shame resting on David's conscience in the process.

Imagine what could have happened if David had not chosen to relent and release the situation to God. He would have attacked Nabal and his family. Many lives would have been lost. While David wasn't literally holding a balloon, he undoubtedly *released* one when he entrusted that situation to God. By letting go of his anger and trusting God to handle it, David avoided disaster and experienced God's blessing in return.

We can't control others. We can't control situations. Ultimately, we can only control ourselves and how we respond to what's happening to us and around us.

We can choose stress or joy. We can choose forgiveness over retribution. We can choose love or hate. We can choose grace and peace or hold a grudge.

I'm reminded of a scripture in 1 Peter 1. That's right, we're returning to our old friend, Peter. The one who often put his foot in his mouth. The one who *did* choose retribution over love when he got out his sword and cut the ear off the High Priest's servant who was one of the people about to imprison Jesus (John. 18:10). The one who later that same night denied Jesus three times.

That Peter wrote, "But just as he who called you is holy, so be holy in all you do; for it is written: 'Be holy, because I am holy'" (1 Pet. 1:15–16).

It took me years to understand what that verse was saying. Its instruction felt impossible.

God is perfect. *I'm not.* God is holy. *I'm not. How could I ever be holy like He is?* But as I reflected on this one day, I felt the Holy Spirit ask me my last name.

Murray, I thought.

Yes, but who do you belong to now? He said. *Whose family are you a part of? Who is your Heavenly Father?*

At that moment, I realized what He was saying. In the same way I'm a Murray and have the identity that comes with that name, I'm also a child of God. I am loved because He loves me. I am forgiven because He has forgiven me. I am holy because *He* is holy.

1 John 4:16-17 says, "We have come to know and have believed the love which God has for us. God is love, and the one who remains in love remains in God, and God remains in him. By this, love is perfected with us, so that we may have confidence in the day of judgment; because as He is, we also are in this world" (NASB).

Friend, as Jesus is, so are you. Rest in that truth. Believe it. Giving God a year and choosing joy isn't something you have to do. It's something you *get* to do.

Obeying Him, reading the Bible, giving, praying, loving others, serving others–all of these are things we *get* to do because this Christian life isn't about rules. It's about relationship. It's about desire, not duty. And it's to be enjoyed not endured.

Though we've reached the end of this book, I hope you return to it whenever you need encouragement or to be reminded again of God's truth. I'm so proud of you for taking on this challenge with me. God has wonderful things in store for your future, and it's been an honor to walk with you through these pages.

As you consider the path ahead, this is my prayer for you:

Heavenly Father,

I lift up the person who has read this book. I thank You for their heart to give You a year of their life, trusting in Your faithfulness and goodness. Lord, meet them where they are—whether they are just beginning their journey or have walked with You for years—and remind them that You are always near.

I pray that they would experience Your presence like never before, that Your Word would come alive to them, and that their hearts would be filled with the peace and joy only You can give. Help them to walk boldly in faith, choose joy daily, and release every burden into Your capable hands.

Father, I ask that You would strengthen them for the challenges ahead, encourage them in moments of doubt, and remind them that You are working all things together for their good. Surround them with Your love, guide them with Your wisdom, and empower them by Your Holy Spirit to live the life You've called them to.

As they continue this journey of giving You their time, talents, and treasure, I pray that they would see Your hand at work in their life, opening doors, providing opportunities, and revealing Your perfect plan for them.

Bless them abundantly, Lord, and let their life be a testimony of Your grace, power, and love. In Jesus' name, I pray.

Amen.

GO ALL IN

- Is there a "balloon" you're holding onto that you need to release to God?
- How does your understanding of joy align with the truth of "yielding to God's way"?

- How can you cultivate a lifestyle of choosing peace, grace, and love over stress and retribution?
- Are you living in the truth that you are loved, forgiven, and holy because of who God is? How can that help you live from a place of joy instead of duty in the days ahead?

EPILOGUE

YOUR NEXT STEP

At City Hope Church in Wichita Falls, Texas, we have a saying—"We're a church of next steps."

No matter how long you've been a follower of Christ—whether you're just starting out or you've been walking with Him for decades—we believe God always has a next step for you. He's always inviting every person to dig deeper, grow higher, and press *further* into the life He's planned for each of us.

That's why the last thing I want is for you to read this book, set it back on a shelf, and go on with life as if nothing has changed.

This is a book of next steps. James, the half-brother of Jesus, said it this way: "Faith without works is dead" (Jm. 2:17).

Now, don't misunderstand me—our works don't save us. Salvation is a gift of grace through faith. But we were created to do good works, and those works are evidence of a faith that's alive and thriving.

Throughout this book, I've shared practical ways to take those steps and live out the faith God has placed in your heart. So, what's next for you?

- **Attend Your Local Church**: Be faithful in showing up and worshipping alongside others.
- **Go Through Membership Class**: Learn more about your church's vision and how you can connect to its mission.
- **Get in a Small Group**: Find community with others, share life together, and experience the growth that comes through authentic relationships.

- **Live Generously**: Trust God with your resources and see how He uses your giving to make a difference in the world around you.
- **Serve Others**: Discover the joy of using your gifts and talents to serve within the church and beyond.

If you will take these steps and give God a year of your life, I can promise you this: you will be a different person a year from now. Your life won't be perfect—that's not the promise—but it will be better. Your heart will be fuller, your relationships will be richer, and your faith will be stronger.

And here's what I'm convinced of: if you truly give God a year of your life, you'll find yourself so transformed that you'll want to give Him the *rest* of your life.

So, don't wait. Take the next step today. Trust God with what's ahead and watch as He exceeds your expectations and leads you into the life you were created for.

Your journey isn't over—it's just beginning!

> "And let us run with perseverance the race marked out for us, fixing our eyes on Jesus, the pioneer and perfecter of faith (Heb. 12:1–2)."

As we say at the end of every church service: *Go with God because He is going with you.*

www.ingramcontent.com/pod-product-compliance
Lightning Source LLC
Chambersburg PA
CBHW020241010526
44107CB00039B/1456/J